CAN YOUR
CUSTOMERS
FIND YOU

ONLINE?

*A How-To Guide
to Marketing
Your Local Small
Business Online*

CHARISA JONES PRUITT

Limits of Liability / Disclaimer of Warranty

The author and publisher of this book and the accompanying materials have used their best efforts in preparing this book. The author and publisher make no representation or warranties with respect to the accuracy, applicability, fitness, or completeness of the contents of this book. They disclaim any warranties (expressed or implied), merchantability, or fitness for any particular purpose. The author and publisher shall in no event be held liable for any loss or other damages, including but not limited to special, incidental, consequential, or other damages. As always, the advice of a competent legal, tax, accounting or other professional should be sought.

This book contains material protected under international and Federal Copyright Laws and Treaties. Any unauthorized reprint or use of this material is prohibited.

Dedication

I dedicate this book to my daughter, Tarisa, who inspires everything I do.

My husband, Tyrone, whose hard work, love and support allowed me the time and energy to pursue my dreams and has given me the son I never had in Crishon.

My constant life supporters: my mother Ruth, my father Charles, my sister Charlene, and my grandmother Maggie who have always given me unconditional love and support and believed in everything I do.

My brother-in-law, Ronnie, whom I appreciate for tirelessly supporting his family and has always been a father like figure for my daughter. He's always there when I need him.

My nephews and niece, who I love like my own, Delano, Chaniya, and Dresden.

These are the people that inspire my life every day, love you all.

Charisa Jones Pruitt

Contents

Chapter 4

ARTICLE & EZINE MARKETING - 61 -

Chapter 5

LIST BUILDING VIA EMAIL MARKETING - 75 -

Anyone can master the techniques discussed in this book with the proper time and effort. The key is TIME and EFFORT. Every business owner does not have the time resources available to implement each and every strategy effectively.

Once you review the strategies in this book and know you want to implement them in your business you may choose to contact Charisa Pruitt and her SEO Alliance Team to see if you qualify for their services.

J.P. Marketing, LLC has a very skilled team that partners with your business to analyze your market, learn your consumers, and takes all the necessary steps to optimize your website and insure you are found on the internet.

Call us for a FREE evaluation of your website. We will review your site, look at potential ways to increase traffic to your site and improve the effectiveness of getting visitors to take action. We will then present our findings plus ask a few more questions about growing your business.

Then if it makes sense, we will create a no obligation proposal identifying ways we can help you achieve your business growth. We like to create win-win situations for our clients and ourselves and for this reason we don't work with every business. We only work with clients we know we can help.

Give us a call at 800-385-6475
Or visit us online at
www.SEOAllianceTeam.com

To Your Business Success!

Introduction

The world is changing - it has been for the past two decades. But, now more than ever, if you fall behind the curve and the shift of the current trends, your business is going to suffer. Just look at the number of failing newspapers or collapsed mom and pop businesses out there, regardless of the economic climate.

Whereas in the past, the only way to market your company and successfully grow your business was to put up billboards, send out brochures and buy ad space in newspapers and local cable. The new route to success with any sized business is to utilize the wide array of tools currently available on the Internet.

There are hundreds of them - ranging from the simplest PPC advertising techniques established almost a decade ago by Google and Yahoo! to the most subtle social media outlets that have sprouted up in recent years like Facebook and Twitter.

Regardless of what you use, marketing has changed and whether you are a company that is wetting your feet for the first time in the Internet's massive pool or someone whose online business is currently struggling, effective use of these techniques is going to make all the difference between whether you make it or join the ranks of the businesses that are collapsing all over the world.

Making It Happen

Don't get me wrong, I don't want to scare you. This stuff isn't rocket science (thankfully). However, it is also not as straightforward and textbook simple as the traditional marketing methods you're used to. You cannot just hire someone to write up a brochure and send it out to a half million people, then wait for responses. That kind of blanket approach doesn't work anymore.

This isn't a bad thing though. Luckily, while the Internet has complicated things a bit by throwing dozens of new tasks at you, it has also streamlined a lot of the marketing process. You can target your audience now. Forget about the people who would never buy your product and the money you waste by marketing to them along with everyone else in your city. You can actually create and market your ads to the exact people you know will be more likely to buy your products or services. You can make it so they come to you - that's real power.

And better yet, with analytics you can also measure and check your progress. You can see if your ads are working on a demographic basis. Are the people who search for the keyword "Subaru roof racks" visiting your website and purchasing more often or less often than those who search for "roof racks for Subarus"? That is the kind of control you're going to gain over the marketing process and after a little while, you'll never want to go back. Being able to tweak small pieces of ads in real time, monitor and control your branding over multiple channels, and generally affect how every aspect of your marketing campaign operates is highly addictive - in fact, for some it might be a bit too addictive (but we'll get to that later).

For now, I want to make sure you know that this is not just the wave of the future, but the marketing techniques you should be using right now. This book isn't going to flip your books on their heads, but it will streamline your marketing with methods that have been proven to work by millions of businesses before you.

Get ready to learn what you need to take advantage of the tremendous tools that every single business on the planet, no matter how small or large they may be, should be using and how to start catapulting yourself to the top of the charts for your given niche. Best of luck and here's to your business' future Internet successes.

CHAPTER 1

Getting to Know Online Marketing

Eager to get started? I hope so, because in just a few short pages, you're going to dive head first into the massive collection of tools that businesses have figured out how to turn into recurring revenue streams over the past few years. What's the best part about it all? It doesn't matter if you're a Mom and Pop shop running out of a back lot in the suburbs or a multinational corporation with millions of dollars to throw at the process - the Internet is a tremendous equalizer.

In fact, this book has been written in a way that will make it possible for you to perform the given tasks with little or no money. That's part of the glory of online marketing - it doesn't require a massive pile of capital for investment. It just takes some creativity, a bit of time, and a clear vision for how your business will pull it all off.

With that in mind, let's take a look at what exactly you're going to be doing in the coming chapters and how it's different from what you're used to.

Why Not Traditional Marketing?

The first question every normal business, especially those that have been around for a few decades, will ask, is why the methods they've been using for decades are no longer as viable as the new, online ones. The answer isn't as simple as some would like it to be. First off, the old methods are not dead...yet. If you place a billboard up or spend a few thousand dollars on a radio or TV ad, you'll still get a ton of exposure and your sales will benefit from it.

The problem is that you need to spend those few thousand dollars to make an effective media campaign happen. If you're a big business, it's no big deal. If you're that Mom and Pop shop on the corner, good luck coming up with the funds to pull it off.

When you go on the Internet, money takes on a very different demeanor. Not only can many of the advertising methods you'll read about be done without a single dime, they are generally recommended by the search engine experts as a more effective way of driving traffic. What's the tradeoff? It could take a little longer. If you want to build a website and put it on page one of Google for your keywords, it may take a few weeks for the broader key words, not as long for the more focused keywords. The reward you'll get in increased sales will make it overwhelmingly worthwhile to do so.

The second thing that sets Internet Marketing methods aside from the offline methods you're so used to is the sheer ease with which you can analyze and manage the effect that your actions have on specific demographics. Basically, you can control every little aspect of what you're doing in ways that an offline advertising campaign couldn't even dream of.

Free tools like Google Analytics (which we'll get into later) make it possible to keep track of not only who visits your website, but how long they spend there, which pages they read, what site referred them, what actions they take, what IP address they came from and much more. You can measure and check exactly what actions you're taking that are resulting in positive responses from potential customers in almost every aspect of your marketing campaign. Just try doing that with a billboard; it doesn't have the same effect.

While I could go on for pages upon pages with reasons why Online Marketing is going to change how you market your business, I'd rather tell you about the methods you'll actually be using because I think that after you get an idea of what you'll be using and how you'll be using it, you'll see exactly how your business is about to be changed forever.

Before we go on any further, I want to share what I think are the four cornerstones of Internet marketing - the various methods through which you will build your business and create new interest. Some are familiar and others only vaguely similar to methods you use now, but they will all be used to create interest and make sales.

Search Engine Listings - The Ultimate Goal

The ultimate goal of any internet marketing campaign is to create a good website and to market it in a way that it gets solid search engine listings for multiple keywords. That's the focus of this book – (driving traffic) getting your target market to your website without spending thousands of dollars in advertising to do so.

There are a number of tools you'll use to do this, ranging from writing good content that search engines like (we'll go over this in many forms) to building links from other highly respected websites (time to do some networking).

And while you might read many different tips on the Internet that tell you how to get a good listing for your website organically (without paying), the truth is that the number one thing you can do is create quality content that your readers will be able to use. With algorithms becoming more sophisticated every day and so many websites and search engines locking out sites that are apparently trying to spam their way into good listings, the methods outlined in this book need to be used carefully to ensure you do it all correctly.

A few things you're going to learn about in the coming chapters include:

- ❖ Keyword Research and Selection
- ❖ Niche Marketing - Knowing your audience
- ❖ Content Creation on your Landing Page and Beyond
- ❖ Article Marketing
- ❖ Link Building
- ❖ Testing and Analytics

If it looks like a long list, don't worry. It's not nearly as complicated as it might seem. The truth is that once you get started and put the initial investment of time into your website, you can spend as little as 30 minutes a day on upkeep and optimization to maintain your listing position. As long as you always remember that this is the most important thing you will do, you'll be set.

Some people will want to pay someone else to implement these techniques because they aren't computer savvy, or don't have the time. There's nothing wrong with paying someone else to accomplish these techniques for you. As they say, either do it yourself, or pay somebody to do it, as long as you get it done.

Myself, even if I decide to pay someone else to accomplish certain tasks for me, I like to have a certain level of knowledge so that I'm comfortable that I'm getting what I pay for. If you don't have the funds to pay somebody to do it, which a lot of businesses don't right now in the current economy, I say do it yourself. This book will guide you to do that.

Direct Advertising

The next method we'll be talking about is direct advertising, something you may be a bit more familiar with. However, don't get advertising on the Internet confused with how you do it in the local paper. You will get much more control over your results with the methods we're going to use.

The most effective and widely used of those methods is going to be PPC or Pay Per Click advertising. These are the ads you see on Google or in your email inbox all the time. Basically, someone chooses a set of keywords that they think their customers would search for. Then, they create an ad or ads that will show when someone searches for those keywords and bid for position. When someone clicks on their ad, they will be charged whatever their bid was for that position.

You only pay when someone actually visits your website and you get endless tools to use in measuring and tracking how many people visit, how long they stay, and when they make a purchase. If you're going to spend money in your online marketing campaign this is one of the best ways to do so. However, it is very easy to spend way too much way too fast, so we're going to create a plan that will allow you a quick and easy method to measure and control your clicks, their cost and the ultimate return on investment.

While Google is the biggest with nearly 60% of the market share on PPC advertising, there are others out there. Yahoo! Search Marketing (At the time of this publication, Yahoo! Search Marketing and MSN Adcenter are in the process of merging. Therefore, some of the information regarding each may have changed by the time this goes to print.) is a big chunk on the net with nearly 25% of the market and you'll find that sites like Facebook are extremely viable as advertising locations due to the ease with which you can target traditional demographic groups - something Google and Yahoo! are not as good at.

In the end, if you have a budget to spend, there are a ton of ways to boost your visits and sales with advertising, and a series of steps you're going to learn to get you there.

Viral Marketing

The third leg of the Internet Marketing is almost like a catch all and may seem similar as well. Basically, this is the Internet's version of word of mouth, and is going to be a tool that works extremely well for some businesses and provides only minimal leads for other. Either way, it is a fun and creative way to grow your business online and the possibilities are endless.

Basically, the goal of viral marketing is to create a product or idea that spreads on its own, without any additional work from you. Think of a YouTube video that people email to each other or a funny blog post that someone might want a friend to read. There are dozens of different things that can be done on your part to make a viral product, from creating a free download that is highly useful to your target audience that links back to your website (such as an eBook on how to perform a certain task), or a video that will catch the interest of that audience.

We'll look at a few ways that viral marketing is going to help you attract attention and how your specific niche and business will benefit from these different methods.

Lead and List Building

The fourth cornerstone of Internet Marketing is the most traditional sounding of the bunch and doesn't vary all that much from what you're used to. In this particular instance, it is the building of lists and leads that you can contact again later on.

This can be done in a few different ways, via email lists, newsletters, and services that you may create or integrate into your website. Blogging is another powerful tool that will keep your potential customers coming back and that will always have an impact on them if you can keep your posts interesting and informative (the latter being the most important).

In general, the goal here is to provide something of value to people so they remember you when you come back to them later and try to draw them to your landing page. Whether you're trying to sell a jet ski or a marketing package, the idea is generally the same, but we'll go through a few different variants and methods of doing this later to give you an idea of how your niche can benefit from list building.

Time to Get Started

I won't pretend the paragraphs above cover everything you need to know to create the perfect marketing plan for your website when you first jump online with your business, but I can tell you that it represents the most important aspects of what you'll be doing.

Once you understand what you're getting in to, the next few chapters are going to be that much easier to understand. So, let's get going and start revising how you market your business on the Internet.

C H A P T E R   2

PPC (Pay-Per-Click) Advertising

There are two good reasons why I'm going to start out with PPC advertising. First off, it's often the most misunderstood online advertising option out there. Too many businesses see it as the closest method to what they're used to and start pouring funds into their AdWords or Yahoo! accounts without any research, analytics or testing. That's a bad idea and before we go anywhere, I want to make sure you understand why.

Second, there are tons of ways you're going to be able to start building your online presence without spending mounds of cash in the process. In fact, many of my favorite Internet marketing methods are mostly if not entirely free and so by starting out with the one method that will *always* cost you money, I want to provide a strong contrast between what you can do and what you should do.

Who Benefits

Which leads us to the first question - should you use PPC advertising for your business? It's a bit of a loaded question, mainly because the answer depends so heavily on what kind of business you operate and what kind of funds you have set aside for your marketing campaign.

However, I like to suggest that anyone with a website and a product to sell at least start a PPC advertising campaign through the big two - Google and Yahoo! The tools that these services provide are immensely powerful in a number of ways, both for testing changes you make to your website and for getting quick surges of traffic to your website when you have a new product or a limited opportunity.

However, as I mentioned before, you need to first and foremost know how to use the tools properly so that you don't waste money on ads targeting the wrong people. That's what this chapter will focus on - giving you the information you need to develop a PPC campaign that will work in both small and large increments while being as efficient as possible, regardless of your budget. This isn't flyer and brochure marketing anymore - you have too much control over your ads to start tossing cash around.

The Basics

As I've mentioned already, PPC advertising is the closest thing to what you're used to. In its most basic essence, it is direct marketing - the same method that was used by magazine and quarterly publishers since the 1800s. You send an ad out to a specific demographic, await a response and then use the data of who responds and how they respond to cater your campaign more specifically.

Except, instead of waiting for 6-8 weeks and getting very small sample sizes, PPC advertising allows you to grapple huge groups of people with hundreds or even thousands of ad presentations per hour over a wide array of topics. You can analyze and utilize that data in real time to make adjustments and ultimately pinpoint the ideal customer who will click your ad more often than anyone else and make a purchase. It's all about maximizing the return on investment (ROI) on every single ad you place.

How It Works

A PPC advertising campaign can be started in as little as 5 minutes. You need a landing page of some sort - you should already have a website put together and ready or plan to get one as soon as possible, if you are reading this book - and an idea of who your ideal customer is. You then create an ad that will appear alongside search results for keywords you are going to select shortly.

You will choose keywords, phrases, and circumstances for those searches to go along with the ads you write and bid on those keywords. Every time someone searches for that keyword, your ad will appear in the position you bid for. You don't pay for that appearance. Rather, you pay whenever someone actually clicks on your ad.

So, unlike most advertising methods you are used to where mere exposure costs money, PPC advertising requires that you cater your campaign in a way that will maximize how often a click converts to a sale. This can be done by ensuring only people interested in making a purchase are clicking your ad, and that when they reach your website, they are drawn toward performing a desired action - in this case, buying your product or service.

Why It Can Get Messy

The problem with PPC advertising, as you will see shortly, is that the sheer volumes of people out there that are willing to click on an ad can quickly sneak up on you. Imagine that you are selling Roof Racks for popular SUVs and Wagons. You try to think of a keyword that people who might want to buy a roof rack would click on. You come up with a list of keywords that are fairly specific along with a couple general ones like "roof racks" and "car travel".

Now, imagine how many people type "car travel" into a search engine. It ranges anywhere from 100,000 a month in the winter holiday months to three times that between May and August. If you forget to set limits on your account, you could quickly spend thousands of dollars on clicks for a keyword that will likely not convert to sales of your roof racks. After all, people searching for "car travel" are probably looking for locations, tips, and information about travel, not accessories.

Anticipation of these things is tough, but that's why a PPC campaign needs to be carefully constructed. Starting small, only working with select keywords, doing niche research, and constantly analyzing results will all serve to ensure you never overspend your means or waste your valuable advertising budget on keywords that are never going to convert.

Getting Started

Now that we've gotten the introductions out of the way, let's start dipping our toes into the pool of online advertising options. If you've spent any amount of time on the Internet, you've heard of Google and seen their ads lacquered all over their search pages. The service they use to integrate these ads is called Google AdWords and it is the single largest online advertising platform on the planet. Everyone from Coca Cola to the bicycle repair shop on your block uses Google AdWords and you should too.

However, while Google has over 55% of the search volume in the United States (and similar shares overseas), there are other services out there. Yahoo! has its own search marketing department and with a 25% share of searches, they are an important segment to include. Additionally, Microsoft has their Bing Search service with paid advertising options and there are some smaller guys out there that can provide some specific targeted search for your business.

We'll take a closer look at how Yahoo! and Bing operate in a bit, but for the most part, Google AdWords is the way to go and because it provides the most detailed tools of any online advertising service, it's going to be your go to service for any new ad campaigns. Additionally, most of the things we'll discuss for Google AdWords hold equally true for Yahoo! and Bing. The interfaces may be slightly different, but the application is almost always the same.

Google AdWords

Google AdWords was the first online advertising platform to make use of large scale PPC and as a result, it made Google into a multibillion dollar company with billions in cash stores. The company has built its entire reputation and success on its PPC platform and its long held philosophy to offer as many high tech, free tools as possible to people that will provide them revenue. It is also the oldest of the platforms and the most firmly established.

Better yet, AdWords is incredibly easy to use - however, don't be lulled into a false sense of security because it takes 5 minutes to sign up and start spending money. You need to learn exactly what everything in the platform does if you want to optimize properly and save money effectively.

Signing Up

Signing up for Google AdWords takes no time at all. While you'll want to do some heavy research on your keywords and ad formats before you ever start spending money, the account creation process at least is seamless.

To get started, visit http://adwords.google.com and click on the "Start Now" button located just above the login form. You will now have to create a Google account if you don't have one. Once your account is created, set your time zone and currency preferences. You are ready to create your first campaign.

You will choose your language of choice and how you want to target your ads. There are more than 25 languages available for AdWords (and more added all the time). Additionally, you can choose to target your ads by countries and territories, regions and cities or through a specially customized interface that will work with a particular method you want to employ.

Your business will dictate which is best for you. I recommend you go with one of the first two. If your product is digital and can be marketed anywhere in your source language, use countries and territories. If it is a local business, stick to regions and cities so you don't waste your budget in places that your ads cannot convert.

Next up, Google will automatically have you create an ad to be placed in your profile. For now, just enter information in there as you have envisioned it. We are going to go over this in much more detail soon and create a truly effective ad so don't worry about what it looks like just yet.

Additionally, you will need to choose keywords. This is probably the most important thing you will do for your entire campaign, so just skip it for now. We will definitely come back to this in a little bit (and do a lot more research before picking even one keyword for your campaign).

The final thing that the signup page will ask for from you is your preset budget. While you may already have numbers in mind, we'll talk more about this soon. For now, make sure that your currency is set to USD$, and that your daily budget is no greater than $5 or $10. You're going to want to start small no matter what your end budget is.

There are multiple good reasons for this, foremost being that if you try to boost your budget up too soon, you're going to have a real problem controlling where that money goes. For the default CPC bid (the amount you will pay per click on your ads), enter $0.50. This number might go up if you have a high competition niche, but for now, this is a good baseline for a starter account.

Finally, Google will show you everything you just entered and make sure it is all what you actually want. Review the page carefully to ensure nothing is entered wrong, but don't fret too much. You can change everything on this page later once you have created your account. Finally, you will be able to sign up for your account and get started.

Enter your contact information and then pay for the $5 activation fee. This is not for anything other than to make sure your account is legitimate and that your credit card will work since all ads are billed after the fact. You will be credited for the $5 on your first bill. Now that you are signed up, verify your account via email and login. It's time to start tweaking your ads.

A Look at Your AdWords Account and Tools

Now that you've signed up, it's time for a complete tour of your AdWords profile before we start creating any ads. This is a vital step in the process as you want to be sure that you have a firm grasp of where each tool and report is before you need them. The page you will see when you log in to AdWords provides a good starting point for information. Your current campaigns will be charted along with recent billing, keyword activity and other key bits of information. It's a good window glance of what you're dealing with, but you really need to dig into the tools if you're going to get the most out of your AdWords account.

Opportunities Tab

The Opportunities Tab that Google provides is a sort of automated way to get Google's input on how your campaign is performing and what actions you can take to alter or boost that performance. Ideas are automatically refreshed every two weeks or sooner. You can accept the changes you like and reject changes you don't. This tool will help you keep track of what small tweaks and changes would do you well. If you are having trouble with ads not appearing due to quality scores, this is a great tool to find out why.

It will break down your keyword choices and tell you which ones are effective, which ones are weak and which ones are working properly. It will also give you feedback on ad balance so that you can place more of the successful ads and less of those that are not working properly. Generally speaking, this is a tool that you can use often or never look at and be okay with. If you do use the Opportunities though, make sure that you don't rely on it too heavily, so that you don't start cheating out on doing the hard work in analysis.

The Keyword Tool

Once upon a time, the AdWords Keyword Tool at https://adwords.google.com/select/KeywordToolExternal was not all that great. But recently, it has become a much more useful tool, even if it is not 100% accurate. Basically, what you get with the Google AdWords Keyword Tool is a resource that will allow you to quickly research and understand what you are getting from your keywords. If you need to find new ones, check what data is being provided for existing ones or just do a quick analysis of your choices, this is a good place to start (though other keyword tools you will see shortly are slightly more effective).

To use the tool, enter a list of keywords into the box provided, each of them separated by commas and you will be given data such as advertiser competition (by low, medium and high measurements), search volume by month, year and average, average CPC (cost per click) for the ads, how many clicks per day you can expect, how you will place in listings based on your default CPC bid, and a few other details that are relatively new.

Google has recently added the ability to get an actual number for searches in a given time period, something they did not do for a long time. It is never 100% accurate and you should always remember that keyword data changes from month to month and if the databases do not get properly cleansed the numbers can be inaccurate in many ways. However, these numbers will give you solid baselines for your estimates.

Additionally, the Keyword Tool will also recommend keywords that relate to the ones you search for along with all the data above, and you can add them to your campaign directly from this page.

Ads Diagnostic Tool

If an ad or a keyword for that ad are not displaying properly (Google will tell you when the ads appear and do not), you can run the Ad Diagnostic tool to find out why. This is a quick and easy way to see if there is a problem with your budget, a location issue, or if your quality score is just too low. Just so you don't get confused about what this all means, here's a quick rundown of what quality score means and how you can affect it.

Quality Score (Most Important)

The Quality Score of an ad is the method by which Google measures and analyzes your ads to see if they are a good fit for the keywords you selected. In some cases, Google likes to ensure only viable ads are being placed. They will analyze your landing page to ensure the subjects match, check the average bid prices, and analyze your ad itself to make sure it is a good ad. If the quality score is too low, the ad will be bumped to a lower position or sometimes not even shown at all. Paying the most money will not necessarily guarantee a top placement. An ad with a better quality score and lower bid may place better and pay less per click than an add with a higher bid and a lower quality score. You want to strive for a score between 7 and 8, anything less, try different things to improve it.

The actual algorithm used for this score is still sketchy, but if you have a low score, the two best places to start are with keyword matching on your website (if the keywords you are using do not appear on your landing page, Google will often assume you are misdirecting your ads), and the CPC bid you make. Sometimes you just need to raise your bid to meet the quality minimums for that topic.

Conversion Tracking

Tracking conversions is a huge factor in how your ad campaign will operate. If you are posting ads and none of them are converting to sales, you need to know why and how to change them to boost how much money you make for the money you are spending. To use this effectively, you will need to turn the feature on and then install a small bit of code on to your website.

It usually involves the same basic installation method as you would use for Analytics at the bottom of the landing page you are tracking, right before the </body> tag. Even if your sales go up, you need to know exactly which sales are coming from which ads. If you make 50 sales after putting up your AdWords campaign and only 2 of those sales come from AdWords, you don't want to triple your ad budget only to find that your sales go up to 54 as a result.

Google Analytics

Google Analytics is another service from Google completely unrelated to AdWords but one that will integrate with AdWords if needed and provide you not only with conversion tracking, but extremely detailed analytics about who is clicking your ads, when they do it, where they do it from, how long they stay on your pages, etc. We'll go more into how to use Analytics and how vital it is later on, but for now, just make sure you sign up for an account and install the tracking code on your website.

Yahoo! Search Marketing

I'm not going to get repetitive and drown you out with information about Yahoo! that we just covered with Google AdWords, but you should know that Yahoo! Search Marketing provides similar tools to Google AdWords and a much better keyword tool interface. Unfortunately, they also have a bad habit of trying to up sell you on paid listings and boosting your natural marketing for your website. I recommend you have a Yahoo! account but focus at least 75% of your PPC budget into AdWords where you can get more out of it. Once you have gotten a good feel for keyword selection and ad composition, turn to Yahoo! and start your Search Marketing campaign with the research from your Google campaigns.

Bing Search

Microsoft's Bing Search (adcenter.microsoft.com) makes up around 11% of the market and while the tools provided are high tech and very useful, their tools are not that old, their databases are limited in detail and you're not going to get nearly the same coverage as through Google or Yahoo! If you plan on doing local search marketing, I recommend signing up for Bing as their local options are among the best around, but for universal and international search, you'd do better focusing on Yahoo! and Google.

Effective PPC Campaigns

Now that you've been introduced to the various PPC services out there, it's time to take a closer look at what you actually need to do to be effective with your campaign. This is where all those tools and tabs in AdWords are going to start making sense.

Niche Research

Niche research is the first stop for anyone who is getting their AdWords account underway. Basically, the purpose here is to ensure you understand exactly what your readers are looking for before you jump head first into anything else. Imagine trying to sell sports equipment if you didn't know anything about the sports or the people who played them. This is the same thing. In most cases, you probably already have a pretty good idea of who you're dealing with. However, knowing how those people think and operate on the Internet is a different thing entirely.

Getting to Know Your Customer is step one in any researching process and that means finding out how they talk, what they search for and what content they most often visit.

Who Is Your Customer

Your first stop is to understand who the customer is. Let's take a look at our Roof Rack example again. Let's pretend you're selling Roof Racks for SUVs, Minivans and Wagons. Now, how would you go about finding who your customers are?

Make a List - Start by brainstorming ideas cold. Just make a list of everyone you can think of who might search for the keywords you are providing. You may also create a preliminary list of keywords that we will use soon to do the deeper research.

Search for Keywords - Start searching for keywords that pop to your mind for that particular niche. This is not the same as keyword research - you're just looking to see what other people are writing about for the same keywords and topics. Look at the top sites for those keywords, how the text is written and what topics are of intense interest to the demographic in question.

Look at the Competition - Look at your competitors as much as possible. Later we'll discuss how to use their websites to help in the SEO of your own, but for now just look through everything carefully and get a feel for what other businesses think is important to your demographic on the Internet.

In the case of Roof Racks, you're going to find that the general target demographic is men from 25-40 and families of 3 or more. There are two primary reasons to need a roof rack - for outdoor trips like camping and skiing and for long road trips. In either case, the goal is to find extra storage for items that will not fit in a normally large vehicle. Most individuals are looking to solve a problem and will only make a single purchase - they are not roof rack "fans". They are customers who are educating themselves.

Recording Data

Another thing that can help you here is to start writing down the following bits of information as you research:

How many websites appear for each keyword?

How many ads appear beside the search results for each keyword?

How many links each website on the front page has coming in to it? (to learn this, copy the URL for the website and then type: links:http://www.URL.com into the search box. Google will show you how many links are pointing to that website.)

What is the average cost per click for the keyword? I'll show you this in a moment.

Any special words or language that the industry uses that you may not have thought of - you may know roof racks better than anyone around, but if shorthand is used online to describe it, record it and keep it in mind for your keyword research later.

Keyword Selection

One of the most common questions I get is "what is the difference between niche research and keyword selection?" The truth is that the differences are minimal. However, with keyword selection, you are going to get a few truly powerful tools on your side to help make your decision instead of just observing the other sites out there.

Why not just skip directly to the tools? It's important to get an impartial look with your own eyes at the data before seeing analysis by a third party. If the two synch up, you're set. If there are gaps between what you think and what the numbers tell you, it's time to think about why that is and how you can close that gap.

Who is Searching?

The first thing we'll do is research keywords. You should already have a brainstormed list of keywords to get you started. Luckily, even if this list is only a third complete, you can use free tools on the Internet to complete it.

Google Keyword Tool

The first tool you should use is the Google Keyword Tool. You'll later find that it is not as powerful as you may need it to be, but it will provide suggestions, give you rough estimates of search volume and a good chunk of data to start with. In this case, try entering "roof racks" into the keyword tool.

Check what Google provides as estimates and suggestions for additional keywords. Never just copy and paste Google's lists - that's a quick route to wasting money in your campaign. However, record in a spreadsheet or a notepad the keywords that match your own list.

The goal here is to find keywords that have high search volume and low competition. For example, if you were to look at 'Subaru roof racks" the competition is high and the search volume is only medium. However, if you specified that a bit to "2007 Subaru outback roof rack" the volume drops a bit but so too does the competition. You may want to record that keyword with the data Google provides to do some more research.

Wordtracker

The next tool we're going to look at is actually a paid tool that you can use for free if you sign up for a free trial. The power and usefulness of tools like Wordtracker (www.wordtracker.com) greatly eclipses what Google provides so you're probably going to end up using it more often, however keep in mind the high cost of these tools. Unless you're running a four figure advertising campaign, the chances are that the data you get here in the free trial will be enough.

Wordtracker will sort through databases of information going back weeks and months and provide you with up to date estimates of how often a word is searched for and a much more effective list of suggestions for alternate keywords to match your own. It also allows you to save keywords and look up their data specifically. I recommend you run all your data through Wordtracker, even if you're satisfied with Google's keyword suggestions.

Keyword Discovery

The third tool I want to show you for research is Keyword Discovery (www.keyworddiscovery.com). This is a tool that is much more reliable, but not necessarily any more accurate than Wordtracker. Drawing from over 100 search engines and meta data across the world, it will provide a ton of data for you to sort through about different keywords, demographic data and search trends. However, it also has a free trial. If you want all the bells and whistles you'll need to pay upwards of $600 or $1,800 to access them. The odds are you'll never need those tools though.

Checking Competition

As mentioned above, one of the most effective research tools around is the researching of your competition. If you can look at what other people in your own niche are doing, you can draw from their data and use it for your own devices. While you've already searched Google to see what your competition is doing, I want to show you a much more effective tool that will help you out in determining what you'll be paying for adspace and if your keywords are worth using.

Now, keep in mind that Google technically offers similar data. But, Google's data is incredibly inaccurate at representing how much you'll actually need to pay for a good position with your keywords. Your goal for each keyword is to:

❖ Appear in the first half of the front page of advertisements (the top 5)

❖ Bid as little as possible without falling out of that position
❖ Find the most cost efficient keywords to use for your campaign

To do this, you need to find keywords with less competition, more search volume, and a good conversion rate from click thrus. You should be starting to see why having 50 keywords in a single AdWords campaign isn't going to get you very far.

Using SpyFu

To find out what your competition is paying for their ads, you can enter a keyword or website into SpyFu (www.spyfu.com) and receive estimates based on cached data of what the current ad count, the current average CPC (Cost-Per-Click) bid is and what you need to reach the top spot for that keyword.

Because AdWords operates almost entirely in real time (there's a short delay, but it's minimal), and users can drop their bids whenever they want, this data is never 100% accurate, but it gives you a very good idea of what you'll be paying for a keyword. You'll get data on the average cost per click, and the change from the previous week, the clicks per day on average, the total cost per day on average, number of advertisers and the total search results for that keyword. All this data changes frequently, but SpyFu has a pretty good database and has been around for a while so their data is trustworthy beyond most other services.

Keyword Types

While researching keywords is all fine and good, you will also need to start figuring out what variations and styles of keywords are going to work best for your campaign. This is another reason Wordtracker and Keyword Discovery are so useful. In Wordtracker, you should search for your term and then do a Lateral or Thesaurus search. This will tell the service to search for keywords that derive specifically from that root keyword. You'll get data on how the keyword operates in multiple forms.

For example, if you typed "Subaru Roof Rack", it might spit out "Subaru Roof racks", "Roof Racks for Subarus", "Subaru accessories", "Subaru Outback Roof Racks", and more. Each one of those results will contain the current estimate of searches per month, an estimate for the next month (based on historical data) and an option to dig deeper and find even more data (for paid subscribers).

Variant Types

There are multiple variants of keywords you may decide to use. Keep in mind that each iteration of a word is considered different by the search engines. If you pay for an ad with "Roof Rack", you will not appear for "Roof Racks". For that reason, you need to think carefully about what will be searched for. Here are some options to include in your research:

Plural - Adding or subtracting a plural is always something you should do for every keyword you research. See what the differences are and if they are the same, just do both.

Misspellings - Many times, especially with commonly misspelled words, having misspellings in your keyword list can be advantageous. Google has gotten better at catching these, so you should be wary of losing views, but names and places especially can be good for this.

Variants on Language - If you're writing an ad in English from Missouri, the same words might be spelled differently in Canada, England or Australia. If your product can be sold internationally, make sure to check for alternate spellings.

Alternate Names - If something has more than one name or is called different things (this is where your niche research comes in handy), make sure to check all versions.

Slang - On the Internet especially, slang can be a big factor. Shortened words, street talk, or demographic specific language is always important and should be researched.

Abbreviations - When selling anything technical, look for any abbreviations. For example, a part on a car might be searched for by its part number alone. You should research that keyword along with the full name.

Long Tail Keywords

While the variants above can be effective in pinpointing different forms of your keyword, one thing you need to also keep in mind is long tail keywords. A long tail keyword is a keyword based on your base keyword that combines multiple additional words to make it more specific. The most common situation in which someone might use these is for local business, when your customers will more often search for your product along with a location.

For example, if you were a local mystery bookstore in San Francisco, having ads appear for "mystery bookstore" would be useless because you want people to appear in your store. So, instead, you would use long tail keywords such as:

Mystery bookstore in San Francisco
Mystery bookstore near San Francisco
Mystery bookstore in the Castro
Mystery bookstore in the bay area
Mystery bookstore in or near Castro San Francisco

As you can see, the possibilities are endless. Many times, for local businesses especially, the lists of long tail keywords that might be tacked on to an ad stretch on for dozens of lines. Don't worry about how this affects your budget though because even if each keyword only gets one search a month, when you add them all up, you'll have a viable strategy that will ensure you are hyper targeting your audience.

Keyword Matching

One thing that Google and most other PPC services allow is for you to designate how your keyword will be matched. You can choose to have an exact match where your ad will only show when the exact keyword is searched for (indicated by placing [brackets] around a keyword), you can choose to have your ad show for any search that contains your keywords (keyword alone), or a phrase match (indicated by placing "quotations" around the keyword). For long tail and specific keywords, the best route is probably going to be exact matching, but if you want to broaden your approach or if your keyword can appear in different forms, the latter is a good idea. However, if you ever do broader matching, always consider the following:

Negative Keywords

The final thing I want to touch on with how a keyword is formed and researched is negative keywords. Negative keywords are a very important aspect of every PPC campaign as they allow you to exclude words from your ads.

If you were selling roof racks for Subarus and you set up a broad match keyword for your ad that was "Subaru roof racks", you might think that anyone who searches for those words would be interested in buying them, but consider the following searches:

Installing Subaru Roof Racks
Removing Subaru Roof Racks
Dealer Subaru Roof Racks
Painting Subaru Roof Racks

These are just a few examples of how the keyword might be entered into a search engine. None of these four searches would result in you making a sale and might just eat up clicks on your ad - wasting your money. So, PPC services like AdWords will allow you to enter words you want to exclude from broad matches. To add negative keywords to an ad or keyword, just place a "-" before the word in your keyword list. For example, a short keyword list would look like this:

[Subaru roof racks], -installing, -removing, -dealer, -painting

This would tell AdWords or Yahoo! to show your ad for any phrase containing "Subaru Roof Racks" but not those searches that include "installing", "removing", "dealer", or "painting". This is an absolutely necessary step if you want to boost you conversion rates.

Split Testing

Split testing is the process of taking a small part of an original ad and changing it slightly, then testing it against the results of the first ad and seeing which performs better. Get used to the process because you'll be doing a lot of it if you want your ads to be as effective as possible. The same goes for your landing pages and most of the other marketing methods you'll use in this book.

For PPC advertising though, split testing is relatively simple, even if it is almost never ending. To get started, you should begin your campaign with two ads. Make sure they are very similar. I recommend using the same headline and only changing one line at a time. Make sure the message remains the same and just change the format used to display that message. Here's an example of two ads:

Subaru Roof Racks (Headline)
All models and types (Description Line 1)
Great for skiing and road trips (Description Line 2)
http://www.SubaruRoofRacks.com (Display URL)

Subaru Roof Racks
Models from 1990 to 2010
Great for skiing and road trips
http://www.SubaruRoofRacks.com

As you can see, the ads are almost identical and even the part we changed is the same in its message. However, we changed the second line in the second ad to be more specific, with actual years. Now, we will run these two ads at the same time, alternating them evenly with the same keywords. This will ensure that the data we get is as close to the same as possible. Make sure to take a large enough sample size though. Running a pair of ads for only a day is not enough data. You need to run them for at least 3-4 days or 1000 impressions each. With that much data, you can start seeing which ad is more effective.

In this case, the latter ad is going to be more effective with its slightly more specific numbers. Upon seeing this, you can start tweaking other parts of the ad including the URL, the headline, and the second description line. The tweaking process should never end, even when you get your ad to perform with higher conversion and ROI (Return on Investment) numbers.

Terms to Know

There are a few terms that you're going to need to know to be effective with your PPC campaign. Here are a few of the more common ones:

Impressions - The number of impressions you get on an ad is how many times that ad is shown by Google. This number has nothing to do with how much money you spend, make or convert. However, it does help you figure out how effective your ad text is at grabbing attention. To get an impression, your ad needs to appear on the front page. This means that if there are 20 people bidding on a keyword and you are not in the top 6-8 you will not get any impressions as you'll be on page two or three.

Click Thru Rate - The Click Thru Rate of your ad is the frequency with which your ad is clicked on when it is shown. For example, if your ad has 1000 impressions and 25 people click on it, your click thru rate is 2.5%. A good click thru rate is one that will utilize your entire budget each day without wasting any hours. For example, if your click thru rate is only 1% but you get 10,000 impressions a day, you are still getting 100 clicks a day - a substantial number of clicks to work with, especially if you can raise your conversion rate.

Cost Per Click - The cost that you pay for your clicks on average is the CPC or Cost per Click. This number will change throughout the day depending on who else is bidding. Keep in mind that people select key hours to show their ads, so you don't have the same competition every hour of the day. As a result, sometimes your cost per click will be higher, usually earlier in the day.

Conversion Rate - The conversion rate is one of the most important numbers in your campaign. This is the percentage of people who click on your ad that make a purchase after clicking through. If you have a high click thru rate (CTR) without any conversions, you are not going to make any money. In fact, this is even worse than a bad CTR because now you're paying for those clicks and getting nothing out of them. A good conversion rate is one that will eclipse how much you are spending on ads. This might be anywhere between 3% and 12%. Usually a good conversion rate is anything above 4% though.

Return on Investment - When you toss all of the numbers above into a blender and mix vigorously, you get this number, the Return on Investment (ROI). Your ROI is going to be the percentage of money you make greater than what you spend. This needs to be a positive number to represent any kind of success in your ad campaign. Keep in mind that the first few days of your campaign may end up with a negative number regardless. That's why we start small, with only $5-10 per day to ensure you don't blow your entire budget in two or three days of poor advertising.

5 Tips to an Effective PPC Campaign

If you follow the steps listed above and measure your success carefully, you will be able to create a good PPC campaign relatively quickly - sometimes as early as within a couple days. However, if you want to maintain that campaign, you will need to ensure that you keep a close eye on a few key factors.

Effective Budgeting

I've already mentioned that you should start your campaign at $5 or $10 but you will need to remain vigilant in measuring your budget as you go forward. Some companies spend $100 a month and others $10,000 on AdWords and sometimes reap the same rewards from those budgets.

You need to be sure that whatever you spend; you don't over saturate your ads. Make sure that there is room for growth by constantly tweaking the amount you spend until it is at the highest point. While the numbers will never be steady, if you change the budget once a week and then measure your success, you can start analyzing the best possible range.

For example if your ROI at $10 a day is 12%, you need to be sure it stays at or above that number as you raise your budget. If you start spending $50 a day and your ROI drops to only 8%, you're now making less money for your investment - you're still in the black, but less so than before. That money might be better spent elsewhere.

CPC Tweaking

Another tip that you should use if you are going to effectively keep your budget under control is to constantly tweak your CPC for every keyword. While there is a default CPC that will automatically apply to every keyword you select, you can manually edit each of them (and should). Here is my process for finding the perfect CPC for each keyword:

Start higher than the minimum - By starting a bit higher than the minimum that Google requires for that keyword to appear on the page, you can build your quality score. When an ad appears for a while, it automatically acquires a higher quality score and will allow you to lower your bid later on - not by a lot, but every little bit counts. Aim for about 25-50% higher than the minimum for 1-2 weeks.

Lower by 5-10% - Start by lowering your bid towards the minimum by 5-10% after two weeks and then watch it for a week to see if your quality score drops or if your results weaken at all.

Edge Lower and Lower until your Quality Score Dips - Continue doing this every week for each keyword until the Quality Score lowers or your ad stops appearing.

Adjust weekly until set - Adjust carefully until the ad appears in the top 5 for your keyword at the lowest possible CPC.

Keyword Selection

Keyword selection doesn't end after your initial research. While some niches might be steadier than others, others might be seasonal (think of flower delivery or certain sports), so you should be regularly adjusting and changing your keywords. For example, if you operate a sports equipment store, you wouldn't advertise for "2010 snowboard models" in July.

Rather, you'd advertise for "2010 surfboard models" up through September and then switch over in October or November for snowboards. You might consider having seasonal keyword lists that you maintain off of AdWords. I like to use a separate spreadsheet where I can make notes of what months and seasons certain words work best for different campaigns. Don't rely too heavily on the tools Yahoo! and Google give you.

Proper Data Usage

The thing about data is that just having it is not going to get you anywhere. You need to know how to properly use that data once you have it. So, to effectively create and maintain your account, don't gorge on data too much.

Do this by selecting only small sets of keywords for each campaign, not checking data for all campaigns at the same time (hence rotating weekly schedules) and not trying to take too much away from the different types of data that Analytics and AdWords provides for you.

Additionally, make sure to get good data by spreading out the appearance of your ads. If you only show ads for three hours a day during weekdays, you are cutting out huge chunks of data that can be used to analyze how they perform. Additionally, always set realistic and effective bid prices so that you get data from good ad positions. Never place ads in the number 1 slot as the number 2 and 3 slots tend to statistically do as well if not better for some keywords, but also stay away from number 5 or 6.

Ad Quality and Creation

The final thing you should maintain in a good AdWords campaign is the utilization of the right ads. Writing a good ad starts with knowing how to say what you need to say in a small space. If you've used Twitter, you have some practice in this. If not, it's time to get some.

Headline - Your headline should be short and to the point with a keyword in it. Capitalize the first letter of each word (but not every letter in the headline). The headline is automatically bolded so make sure to take advantage of that by not being vague.

First Line - List one or two features and if you can, include numbers. If not, be specific about features and don't boast. Using words like "best" are not good ideas as they will often times be ignored immediately.

Second Line - Write at least one or two benefits of your product. Benefits sell better than features as they talk directly to the audience. Make sure you list benefits that match with the specific keywords you are marketing towards so that it is more personalized.

URL Line - For your URL, always list it as simply and easy to read as possible. For multi-word URLs, capitalize the first letter of the words between "www" and ".com"

Combine these tips with the testing methods listed above to make sure that you are doing as much as possible to tweak and perfect how your ads look and perform.

CHAPTER 3

Local Advertising and Classifieds

This next step is going to be one that only a few years ago was not quite as viable as it is today. While services like the Yellow Pages and Google Maps have been hitting the Internet for quite some time now, there were minimal options out there for those looking to maintain a presence online that would specifically target local customers and citizens.

That has all changed in the last few years as services like Google Maps, Yahoo! Local, and Craigslist have become the premiere ways to promote your business locally without spending adverse amounts of money for services you don't need. The best part is that most of the local advertising methods out there can be done for free, allowing you the freedom you need to integrate a full blown advertising campaign into your business plan without having to shell out thousands of dollars a month for PPC or other paid advertising.

How Local Advertising is Different from PPC

The first question that most business owners are going to have of course is what differences there are between PPC and local advertising. Advertising is advertising, right? Luckily for you, the answer is no.

While PPC advertising allows you a great deal of control over who sees your ads and how they search for them, it doesn't integrate as well into the local search arena. For one thing, you need to use keywords to designate how a PPC ad appears. That means that you would always need to include local keywords to designate a specific area in a way that doesn't confuse them with other cities. For example, typing "Portland car care" wouldn't necessarily be an effective strategy because there are multiple Portlands - including two major cities in Oregon and Maine.

However, the tools being provided by the very same companies that make PPC possible, such as Google, Yahoo! and Microsoft are now making local search options much more viable to speed up this kind of search.

What Works

The key is the mapping technology being used. By integrating businesses directly into map services like Google Maps and drawing data from multiple databases including reviews, business locations, contact numbers and photographs, optimization becomes possible in a way that will make it possible to dynamically boost your presence for given keywords.

For example, were you to type "Portland car care" into Google Maps, you'd get a series of results from across the country. The map would zoom out as much as necessary to show you the different results. You can then zoom in to the city you are searching for, let's say Portland, Oregon in this case. By specifying that you want Car Care in Portland, Oregon, you now zoom into that particular city and will see results posted for specific car care locations in Oregon. Atop the listings is a sponsored listing, another feature made possible with integrated paid advertising into the local search options.

However, as you can see, it is possible to appear for free as one of the standard listings for those keywords. There are a number of factors involved in how that works, all of which we'll go into later.

What Local Search Provides

Keywords, business names, review content, volume of reviews, and your location will all have an impact on what appears for your searches - and so you will need to do a lot of tweaking to get your business properly situated.

The best part though is that local search is new enough that many niches and business types are not yet overwhelmed with results. While searching for a type of restaurant or hotel will probably land you with thousands of results, you're not going to find as many "bicycle repair shops" and so optimizing won't be quite as hard.

Another factor which we'll discuss more in depth later is the integration of mobile search in recent years to these types of local optimization techniques. With smart phones becoming more common place (iPhones and Blackberrys), services that integrate Google Maps and other services with local search into the phone are also becoming more popular. Some people might solely search for businesses on their phone now to save time.

Think of local search as the Phone Book of the 21st century. If you want to put your name out there, you need to optimize to appear as early and as readily as possible when someone searches for your business type.

The Different Players

Also like PPC advertising, there are many different resources you can utilize for your local search plan. However, unlike PPC advertising, I'm not going to recommend that you only use one of them. For an effective local search plan to work, you should optimize for all four major local search platforms along with a few other resources that are going to make your business more effective.

Google Maps

The biggest name in local search right now is Google Maps, largely because of the search giant's existing market share. Additionally, Google Maps appears on many of the top selling smart phones out there, integrating the search functions into mobile devices. This is a huge factor that you'll find will become a bigger and bigger part of the online marketing scene in the years to come.

Getting Started

Google Maps is easy for many businesses to get started with because if you are an existing business, the odds are that you are already listed. Google draws a great deal of its listings from various Yellow Pages directories from throughout the country, so the real task here is to go in and claim your business from them.

Google Places

To get started, search for your business in Google Maps. If it appears, find and click on the button to claim the business. If it does not appear, you will need to go to the Google Business Solutions page. When you first arrive in the Business Center click on "Google Places" and claim your business. You need to enter your information. Check any existing listing to ensure it is accurate. Also, make sure to fill out as much information as possible.

People don't just browse the Internet for info any more. They get their contact information and in the case of mobile search, they will call you directly from this listing. If your phone number is wrong, your hours are not listed or you forget to update your address after a move, you'll lose business.

Another important thing you should do here is to update your business description with as much detail as possible. You will need to be specific here. Don't enter general terms like "car parts". This will never get you listed highly for your keywords. Instead, enter something like "car travel accessories supply and installation". Not only is that incredibly specific, it includes multiple keywords that would appear in a search for roof racks.

Additionally, check to make sure your business appears in the right location on the map. Google uses NAVTEQ to get their maps right and if you're in an urban area, it should be accurate, but if you're in a smaller town or an awkward corner of your city, the map can occasionally get you wrong. It's easy to move the marker though and set it right.

Select your category next and make sure you match it correctly. If you can, match to multiple categories so that you show up for more than one search if someone does a general browse for that category.

Tweaking You Listing

Photographs are a great option now as well, something that you should always do if you have a physical location. Set your logo or a storefront photo as the premiere picture (the one that appears with your listing). You may then choose up to 10 additional photos to include as a portfolio of sorts to broadcast your business.

Additionally, if you choose, you can add video links to your listing via YouTube. Local news stories, a tour of your business, or an introduction from yourself are all great things to link here. Too few businesses take advantage of the media options located in many local search databases.

Everyone wants to see pictures - we think visually - and that means this is a must do.

To validate your listing when you finish up adding all the information, you will need to go through and enter an address or phone number you can use to verify the listing. Google will call you directly if you choose the phone option. If you choose a postcard, it can take up to 4 weeks to get the card in the mail with the code you'll need to enter into Google Places. After verification is complete, you'll be able to access and edit your posting whenever you like from Google Places.

Coupons

Google has a cool feature in Google Places that you can use to add a bit of incentive for anyone that happens to stumble upon it. You can set up coupons through here that will allow you to provide discounts both off and online to your customers. Just add a coupon code and a description of the coupon. Make sure it is enticing and always include either a number or the word "Free" in the description to gain the right amount of attention. These can then be printed by customers from the listing and brought into your retail location for the discount you've offered.

Sponsoring Your Listing

You can also sponsor your listing, using your local listing (the information that appears by default in the Google Maps interface), through the Business Center. It will allow you to get more exposure and grow your total hits as you rise to the top of the listings for your keyword. Make sure you review the competition in your keywords though, as it might cost you a good deal if you are up against bigger, larger budgeted campaigns.

Yahoo! Local

Yahoo! Local is the second largest search service and actually has a far greater reach than Google in terms of raw exposure because of the massive size of Yahoo!'s content network. Unlike search engine optimization and PPC, you don't ever choose between which one is best for your business when optimizing for local search - you just do both.

With Yahoo!, getting listed is far faster and much simpler than with Google. Additionally, tool sets are equally as effective and in some cases have more options than the larger company.

Getting Started

To get yourself listed in Yahoo! Local, visit the homepage at http://local.yahoo.com. As you can see, Yahoo! has done a tremendous job of integrating its entire content network into local search. This is a great thing for you because that means there are nearly 50 million people looking at it every day and you can pop up nearly anywhere. Everything from categories to reviews, to events and social networking is connected into a single interface in the Local hub and Yahoo! makes it incredibly easy to plug into it.

To get started, you will need to get familiar with "My Local", the profile homepage for every user on Yahoo! Local. Here, users can see all their reviews, their collections of places and items, topics they have entered in the community forums, and comments they have left or received. Create your own account here and start seeing how it works. The more easily you can understand how the Yahoo! Local interface is used by visitors, the easier it will be to convince them to visit or comment on your business.

Yahoo! Local Search Marketing

Unlike Google, which does free (and slow) submission alongside the work it does to gather websites manually, Yahoo! offers submission services through Search Marketing (the same as their PPC service). You will find that there are multiple options here including basic, enhanced, and feature listings:

Basic Listing – This listing will provide all the same information you did for your Google Maps listing, and put you in the basic directories. No matter what you decide to do in the long run, start by doing this, getting your company listed in Yahoo!'s local directories. This is the free listing.

Enhanced Listing - The next jump up for Yahoo! allows you to post a tagline, a longer business description and 10 photographs for $9.95/month. It is recommended that you take advantage of this service, even though Google offers the same for free. Those pictures are incredibly important to how you present your business online.

Featured Listing – The final option is the sponsored listing option. You can get to the top of the list this way with guaranteed appearance on page one, broader exposure in multiple categories, and a wide array of other features that may be worth it for a larger business or one in a crowded market (small businesses or rural businesses should ignore this option as it is probably unnecessary). The price for this varies based on the locations and how many areas you want to cover.

Once you have entered your basic information, as discussed in the Google Maps section, you will need to ensure that all of your text is properly optimized with the keywords you have selected already for your Google account. Choose your categories next (fill in all 5 of them), and make sure your business appears properly on the map.

When done, you need to verify your listing with Yahoo! To do this, you will just need to approve the terms of service and verify the email you receive. It takes almost no time whatsoever. Before your listing will appear, the site must be reviewed and verified by the Yahoo! team. Depending on your category and the amount of other submissions, this can take anywhere between 3 days and 3 weeks. If you pay for an enhanced or featured listing you will appear immediately without verification time.

Bing Local

The third local search option out there is Bing Local, Microsoft's version of local search and in most cases the best platform out there. Unfortunately, with Bing Local you are only getting an 11% share of the search traffic on the Internet and 0% of the mobile searches. This is a problem for any company that is trying to reach as wide an audience as possible. However, if you have set up and are happy with your Google and Yahoo! profiles, the next step is to move to Bing.

Signing Up

To get started, visit http://local.bing.com and take a look at the page. You will notice that there is no option to login and add your page. This is because the listing center has been hidden away for some reason. The link to reach the listing center is:
https://ssl.bing.com/listings/ListingCenter.aspx. When you get there, you'll need to login with your Live ID if you have one. Otherwise, check the "Add new listing" button and enter the information you have already entered for Yahoo! and Google one more time.

Like Google, many times the information for your business will be pre-populated. When you enter your business name, Bing will try to find it in the InfoUSA and Acxiom databases where that information is gathered and kept. If yours is already available, you simply need to claim it and edit any information that is not accurate.

Tweaking Your Account

Like Google and Yahoo! upload your 10 photos immediately, including a storefront or company logo to show up with your listing immediately. Finally, add the additional detail that Bing allows you to enter that many other search engines might not. You will get a tag line for free as well as a longer then normal company description that you can load down with keywords (and should). Also, enter brands you carry (great for keywords), and any languages you speak to reach multi-lingual audiences.

When you're done, choose your categories, review your listing and then approve the terms of service. Like Google and Yahoo!, Bing will review your listing and get back to you when they have approved it (usually between 1 and 3 weeks).

Yellow Pages and Local Portals

The one thing that many local businesses struggle with is how the offline methods of local advertising translate to the Internet. Even the advertising companies themselves have issues with this one. In the past, the Yellow Pages were a must for any business offline. You needed to be listed to stand a chance of someone randomly happening upon you.

Today, while there are still Yellow Pages and directories on the Internet, they are not nearly as powerful as they were offline. That isn't due to the nature of the Yellow Pages - it has more to do with the companies that run them. Online Yellow Pages should definitely be used, but the exorbitant costs they charge for premiere listings are just plain unnecessary for all but the most competitive businesses. Here are a few of the players out there, including both the

Yellow Pages sites and the Local Portals that are usually free and more effective.

Yellow Pages Sites - YellowBook.com, YellowPages.com, DexKnows.com, etc.

These sites are all generally the same in that they cost money to get anything more than the most basic listing. However, one thing you do gain here is that many of them like YellowBook and DexKnows will integrate offline and online listings into a single account - it makes managing your listings much easier. Additionally, usually listings in these websites will update to other local search engines automatically as this is where they draw their data.

However, the market share of these sites has been falling for some time and the cost of a listing is seemingly unnecessary when you can just as easily get a free listing and optimize in Yahoo!, Google or Bing. If you are going to go with a Yellow Pages site though, DexKnows has one of the best utilized sites online (and a huge advertising budget to back it up).

For any of these services though, online integration is minimal. You'll need to call them directly and deal with their advertising departments if you want to be listed. If it's in your budget, check it out - if not, let's take a look at some of the other local portals that are generally free.

Yelp

Yelp (www.yelp.com) is one of those websites that has popped up more from word of mouth than anything else in recent years, becoming a highly popular local hub of information. It is very similar to a mixture between sites like InsiderPages and Facebook, combining social networking concepts with the local search aspects that so many different websites have been integrating in recent years. The review data that gets populated in Yelp is also used to fill in the reviews on Google Maps and other local search platforms, one of the premiere ways that SEO is performed in local search.

Using Yelp

When you first visit Yelp, you'll notice that the page is full of a number of different features. There are reviews as well as user profiles and business discussions allowing users to communicate with each other about places they like, what they recommend, etc. It's a great way to get involved with your customers as well.

Start out by signing up for a Yelp account. There are two different kinds of accounts - one for personal and one for business. If you already have a personal account, you should upgrade it to a business account before posting so you can keep your profiles separate. This will allow you to talk with other people about your business without seeming to be advertising. You will also be able to keep your own reviews from seeming biased this way. The last thing you want to do is make people judge your business based on your personal tastes.

Make sure to fill in the entirety of your profile with all the information requested and to review it all before posting. Errors here can keep you from appearing in Google results. Once you signup, make sure to check and see if your business already exists. Sometimes it will already be in there from a customer adding it so they can write a review. If that is the case, you may want to claim it directly and then clean up the profile it has to match your brand image.

Leveraging Yelp

Yelp is one of those services (and there are dozens of them) that will require you to keep a bit of an eye on it. The best way to do this is to watch your listing in Google Maps. As you get reviews on the various Local Portals out there (see the list below), you should open profiles on those services and edit your business or claim it accordingly.

The main thing to watch out for with Yelp is the reviews and how they are formatted. You don't just want good reviews - you want well written, concise reviews. While you cannot control what people write about your business, you can encourage customers to write reviews if they are pleased with your service. Have cards that you provide to customers in your store that ask them to go and review your services on Yelp or other review sites. Create a prefilled form that they can write out so that they have enough information to create a solid review.

Insider Pages

Insider Pages (www.insiderpages.com) is another service similar to Yelp, but without so many of the social networking aspects. Rather, it is built more around a traditional marketing angle and therefore you need to think in the form you know best - as a business owner. Make sure to check all information as you add it, take full control over what your profile looks like and how it operates and always double check the map (sometimes someone else could have entered your business in improperly).

There is a special offers menu similar to the coupons in Google maps as well as a special marketing message section that you should always take advantage of. Both of these features will ensure you get your message out to your readers in good order.

Craigslist and Backpage

Craigslist and Backpage are the two premiere classified websites on the Internet and they're both free, something you're not going to find in the local paper. For the most part, the two sites operate in the same format. They are broken down into various cities and metro areas. In the case of Craigslist, all of the pages are operated by the same San Francisco office. For Backpage (www.backpage.com) some of the larger metro pages are operated or prefilled by classifieds from local newspapers such as the Seattle Weekly or Miami New Times. These pages are going to be the same as the rest but with additional classifieds automatically added from those local papers.

Regardless though, there is a tremendous amount of potential waiting to be tapped in these classified portals. Craigslist currently ranks 26th on the Internet in traffic with millions of hits daily and over 12 minutes per day spent by each user. Backpage doesn't have quite the same reach but still averages in the top 1400 websites with over 6 minutes per day from its visitors.

The Difference From Newspapers

In short, these sites are very popular and people spend time on them. Unlike a normal newspaper classified, people visit these sites just to see what's there and if you can be creative and promotional enough, you can put yourself in front of their eyes in ways that will draw attention, cost you nothing, and ultimately build your business.

First off, the speed of these sites is a major factor. If you post an ad at 10am, you can have inquiries by 10:01am and new sales by 10:30. Second, the ease of use is outstanding. Craigslist costs nothing in most sections and takes only a minute or two to post new ads. Both sites allow pictures to be uploaded, and Backpage even allows you to add maps from Google so people can see where you are.

Because both sites are very much the same, we're just going to look at the big one of the pair - Craigslist - but don't neglect to check out Backpage as well as it is a very viable classified source and even has a few neat tools that Craigslist is lacking.

Getting Started

To get started, go to Craigslist (www.craigslist.org) and take a look around the page. You'll notice that there are dozens of different cities and regions listed. Find your own and click on it. If you do not live in a major metro area, click on your state and look for a region that you can work with. Keep in mind that some businesses may not be able to benefit as much from these sites if they are in rural areas from which doing business far away doesn't make sense. However, most businesses will find at least a minor audience to promote to.

Now that you've found your specific Craigslist, it's time to take a look at the nine sections provided by the site. Here is a rundown of each:

Community – People get together and talk about everything from politics to volunteering, to getting to work together. If you are holding a promotion or special event, this is a good place to post an ad.

Personals - You can safely ignore this part of the site as it is designated for finding dates and similar encounters.

Housing - The housing section of Craigslist is one of the biggest. If you're a real estate agent or a landlord, you should be posting your listings or vacancies here. You can also post here as a For Sale By Owner.

For Sale - This part of the website is a mixture of ads from just about everyone out there trying to sell things - from college students who need a few bucks to grandmothers cleaning out old boxes. To keep from being flagged as a spammer, make sure you think small, posting only every couple days or so and always posting specific products from your business. Never post an ad such as "Jim's Car Accessories - Best Deals in Syracuse". It will get flagged.

Services – If you're interested in promoting yourself though, the services section is a great place to do that. You'll find listings here for every type of job imaginable and people promoting the heck out of their businesses. Some areas get read more than others so make sure to check out what other people are writing in your category before posting.

Jobs – If you're trying to hire someone, this is a good place to start. Postings here start at $25, depending on the area, and you'll get hundreds if not thousands of responses more than in a newspaper ad.

Gigs – Gigs are less formal and can be posted for free. If you have an odd job that needs to be contracted, this is where to do it.

Resumes - People post resumes here to get attention from hirers. Look here if you're interested in finding someone without paying the $25 fee to post a job.

The next step in the process is to post an ad. When you go to post an ad, the site will ask you what type of ad (choose from the list above), then where to post it. You can create a profile that will allow you to save your location and your normal ad types whenever you login. I recommend doing this since you'll be spending a lot of time on Craigslist.

When you post your ad, you'll need to mark your specific location (this is important for both SEO and anyone searching for your location), with a neighborhood and city. Additionally, make sure to take advantage of the space given to you without getting carried away. You get 50,000 characters, which is upwards of 10,000 words and you are allowed to use HTML, so a posting can be epically long if you so choose. Most listings don't need to be more than a page though if you can help it.

Add images when possible, and always provide some contact information and list credentials and specific products. These things will ensure that people take your ad seriously (trust is a major problem for some on Craigslist).

Optimal Ads on Craigslist

The following methods will help ensure you have the right ad, regardless of your business niche.

The Title

For the title of your ad, there are a few things you need to consider. Not only are you trying to grab the attention of Craigslist users, but more importantly, Craigslist ads are indexed by the major search engines. Since Craigslist is indexed often, a properly optimized ad can appear on Google's first page for one of your major keywords. Decide what keywords you want to optimize in your ad and create your ad around that. Make sure your keyword is in your title.

Price

In most categories that you will post within, you will be asked to post a price with the title in the directory of listings. There are two ways to look at this. If you are proud of your price or think it will draw more attention in conjunction with your title, add it in. However, if it is just a normal price or can be a distraction, don't put it in. You can always place the price in the ad itself where it does less damage.

Posting Description

The posting description can be between 30,000 and 50,000 characters depending on your category and that gives you a huge amount of space to utilize. Most people choose to use simple text in their ad and that is fine as long as it looks nice. However, if you write with big blocks of unformatted text, you're not going to get too many sales. Here are a few things to consider for your description:

Break Up Long Sections of Text - Don't write huge walls of text that no one will want to tackle. Break things up with subheadings, bolded text, and lists.

Create Bullet Points or Key Facts - Bullet lists and facts that you point out are going to break up text and create points of reference for readers.

Use Lots of Numbers where Applicable - Numbers stand out and are easy to understand for most readers. Make sure all numbers you use are important to a customer and not just thrown in for the heck of it.

Use Images to Break Up Text - Images are great but make sure they are useful in the context of your post. Add a storefront picture, pictures of products you are selling or a finished project you have done recently.

Don't Mince Words - Don't babble for pages of text. Say what you need to say and let that be that. You can post endless ads on Craigslist so if the first one doesn't work you can say something else in the next.

Contact Information

Craigslist will ask you for your email address - make sure that you provide something that you are comfortable writing back from. In some cases, you might get as few as 2 or 3 replies but in others, it might be as high as a couple hundred. I often recommend that businesses create a special address for their Craigslist and Backpage postings so that they can easily track those emails.

The Serious Ad

A serious ad is one that is going to get right to the point and tell your audience what you sell and why they should be interested. This is going to be the easiest to write and probably get the fewest responses unless you are offering a tremendous deal. Short, factual posts with details that do the following:

- ❖ Promoting a business in "Services"
- ❖ Selling a branded product
- ❖ Asking for help or trying to develop an event in Community
- ❖ Inviting people to a gathering or a website.

To make these posts effective, don't tell stories or jokes and don't write anything that doesn't directly add value to the product you are trying to sell.

The Creative Ad

Another type of ad you may end up writing (and should try), is the creative ad. This form of ad is one that no one would waste money on in a newspaper but can try at will on Craigslist or Backpage because the ads are free and they can post as many as they want. Extra information about your products, pictures to go with them, novelty HTML coding, jokes and anecdotes all go well into a creative ad that will help to grab attention and make sales. Your goal here is to do nothing more than entertain your readers on their route to performing the action you have given to them (clicking on a website or visiting your store). Examples include:

- ❖ Rant and Raves about topics that will appeal to your target audience and possibly draw them to a website.

- Product pitch lines with jokes or stories that will draw attention in the For Sale section - like a viral message or a clever radio ad.
- Calls to join you or help you in the Gigs or Services section.
- Stories or slideshows about someone or something related to your company.
- Community postings that gather attention with their folksy or entertaining speech.

The point here is that you can be creative, doing just about anything you want and you will draw attention to your ad - the things above are just examples whereas the list of possibilities goes on forever.

Specific Marketing Strategies for Local Search

Now that you have taken a closer look at a wide array of different services and websites that you can use to optimize for local search, it's time to look into what exactly you can do to make those postings stick out the most.

What the Search Engines Look For

While each local search engine has a different set of basic things they look for in their algorithms, they all tend to work in the same manner. Here are a few of the easiest ways to boost your presence in a search engine locally:

Outside Business Data - The more often you show up in outside business data, the more trustworthy your site looks. Google takes data directly from Acxiom, Localeze, and infoUSA databases while Yahoo! and Bing use them to verify their own databases. Check these databases directly and make sure your listings are accurate and that all information provided is the same.

Having a Website - You should probably have a website by now but if for some reason you do not, go and get one.

Google Maps and Yahoo! especially will reward you through their algorithms if you have a keyword rich website that performs well for phrases your customers search for.

Directories - You need to be listed in second tier directories like CitySearch, Yelp, Local.com, and InsiderPages if you want to rank well in Google Maps or Yahoo! Local. They provide reviews and help verify user interest.

Niche Specific Vertical Directories - There are also a number of vertical directories specific to your niche that can help boost your position. Google especially will use them to verify your price range, checkout times and directions. Think of things like TripAdvisor for hotels or restaurants.

Outside Links and References - You will need to appear in top directories to get valuable back links as well. Examples include the Yahoo! Directory, Chamber of Commerce Sites, or DMOZ (Open Directory Project). These are all usually free, non-biased sites you can be listed in as a business.

Proximity - Some search engines rank this and others don't. However, it is still a factor for most and will have a tremendous impact on your listings. Make sure you are in the right location on the map so that people can find you more easily.

Optimizing

There are a few additional things that you can do to help optimize your site for local search and ensure you show up where you should. Here are some tips.

Cross Platform Integration

Google and Yahoo! especially have a ton of services that are closely related to their local search platforms. You should use these services to ensure you get the most out of them as you optimize. For example, Google has Google Checkout that can be added to your website (highly recommended) as well as Google Base to list your products across multiple Google platforms. These services are technically unrelated, but will help grab attention and sometimes even boost your position in universal searches. The same is true for Yahoo!'s huge list of different content networks.

Inbound Links

Google especially relies heavily on inbound links as a ranking strategy. For Local search this is not quite as important but it still holds value. You will need to ensure that you:

Get Trustworthy Links - Links from websites with high Page Ranks and trustworthy content are best. If you get links from bad article sites or useless directories, you may only hurt your position. Look for links to related sites.

Build for Quality - You'll get more out of 5 good local websites than 100 bad national sites. Look for sites that have local keywords, links to your site that are promoted properly, and content that local customers enjoy. This has the added benefit of drawing traffic directly from that site.

Get Some Variety - Make sure all links are related to your topic, but get a few different kinds in there. Reviews on Yelp, listings in YellowBook, and direct links from local blogs can go a long way in boosting your position.

Reviews

The biggest thing you can do for a website in local search is to get reviews for it. While not every review will bump a site up in the listings (some sites with 20 reviews might show up on page 5), if you follow all the above tips, the reviews you get will have the biggest impact. Quality is important, but quantity cannot be wholly ignored on this one either. Try to get as many reviews as you can. As mentioned earlier, ask people to review your service, either with cards at the storefront or by calling or emailing them directly. It takes no time and it will result in a tremendous boost in business (assuming you get good reviews of course).

Reviews can be submitted directly through Google, Yahoo! and Bing, and if you can get someone to review through the search engines themselves, it's all the better. However, an outside resource will be picked up by the search engines fairly quickly in most cases, so you can also just ask them to write a review on Yelp or any other site they frequent. These reviews are syndicated rapidly.

Common Review Sites

Here is a list of review sites that Google uses to draw its syndication from. Yahoo! and Bing may use other sources but most of these will appear throughout all local search engines:

10best.com
Aol.com
ChefMoz.org
Citysearch.com
Dine.com
DiningGuide.com
Dinnerbroker.com
Frommers.com
Gayot.com

Giatamedia.com
Greenopia.com
Holidaycheck.com
Hotelchatter.com
HotelGuide.com
Hotelguide.net

Insiderpages.com
JudysBook.com
Menupages.com
Mytravelguide.com
Priceline.com
RestaurantRow.com
Travelocity.com
Travelpost.com
Tripadvisor.com
Virtualtourist.com
Yahoo.com
Yelp.com
Zagat.com

If you are in a specific industry such as travel or restaurants, you're going to want to focus more intently on sites that cater to that industry as they syndicate faster and are considered more relevant than the generic sites.

Maintaining a Brand

Your brand is incredibly valuable and unfortunately also very easy to have problems with. Make sure that you keep a close eye on all the resources you are listed through. Signup for accounts on all relevant review sites listed above and check them once every week or two to see if there are any problems. A bad review that is inaccurate or poorly formatted (sometimes, someone might hit 1 star when they mean 5 - it's easy to tell by what they write), can turn into bad publicity.

Protect what people see in your company, review what people are saying and ultimately, ensure that nothing bad comes of anything that is posted on these sites. You have tremendous power over your own image, but you need to exercise it or someone else will take over and do it for you.

Every now and then, your competition may try to slip in a bad review on your business to make their business look better. When that happens, it's usually obvious. Most sites have ways of disputing comments you believe are false, and they're usually resolved quickly.

CHAPTER 4

Article and Ezine Marketing

One thing that many people neglect to consider when they begin marketing their business on the Internet is that there are dozens of different ways through which you can market your website in a way that will not cost you a thing. Later, in the chapter on Search Engine Optimization (SEO), you will learn the importance of back links and keyword integration on your website as tools to make your website show up higher in search listings.

For now, we're going to take a look at one method of optimization that will also gather traffic and attention via content that you're going to distribute. Known as article and Ezine marketing, this method is used by every successful website owner on the Internet and costs much less than some other link building and brand controlling methods. It also helps you maintain the status of an expert in your subject matter and build trust with readers as you lead them to your website to make purchases. Let's take a look at how it all works.

What You'll be Doing

The process may seem odd, but once you get used to it and see what it requires, it makes perfect sense. On the Internet there are hundreds of websites that publish and provide tools to distribute articles written by individuals who want free publicity from those articles. Millions of articles are written on any number of topics and distributed to these sites where they are published with links back to the author's website. No one gets paid and the website places ads on its pages to cover the cost of maintaining the service.

Other users can then come in and syndicate those articles on their blogs, in Ezines, or newsletters that they distribute on their own. The only thing they need to do to use that content for free is to place a resource box at the end of the article with a bio of the author and a link back to the author's website. Basically, it's an automated system to spread your content to other websites and create links.

SEO vs. Readership

One of the primary concerns of this type of marketing is usually to gain links back to your website. Links from highly visible websites are valuable and can help boost your website's ranking for given keywords. However, many times writers will sacrifice quality in favor of quantity and SEO which will then lead to a backlash where readers are unimpressed with the articles. Additionally, whereas many Ezine publishers in the past were willing to publish just about anything, they have started picking and choosing more often what they will publish based on a series of specific criteria.

The reason is that the content is poorly written, stuffed with keywords, and often looks like spam to the search engines. And the last thing any website that plans on sticking around for more than 3 weeks wants is to publish spam.

So, the big question then is whether you should focus more intently on the SEO aspects of the articles you'll be publishing or to aim for readability and interesting content.

There are two ways to answer this question. One, I can tell you that you should always write for readability as that's what the search engines say. Provide quality content and readers will reward you by visiting your site. However, the truth is that if you can find a line in the middle, you can satisfy your readers while also loading up on the benefits of SEO.

But, above and beyond anything else, you should never, ever skimp on quality for SEO. You may not need to write 1000 word articles with research in them, but don't regurgitate garbage content because you will pay for it in the end (and need to write a lot more of it for it to be valuable).

How to Write a Promotional Article

The architecture of a promotional article is relatively simple. While there is no right or wrong way to do it, you are going to need to ensure that a few things remain steady. Here are some guidelines to keep in mind.

General Guidelines

Stick on Topic - Your topic should be steady. Brainstorm a list of topics you think will add to your catalogue of content. No one wants to click on a link for an article about Tropical Fish and end up on a website about Car Accessories. It will backfire in the end, so make sure to write about things that relate to your topic so you can get the most benefit from growing the exposure you're gaining.

Write for Your Audience - Know who your audience is and write for them. Don't write in a way that markets only to a small segment of your audience. Find ways to spread out the content or to hit up multiple aspects over different articles. For example, if your audience is car buyers in their 30s, write about topics that will interest both men and women to ensure you don't leave anyone out.

Be Original - Many websites are starting to turn down repetitive content topics. This can be done in the form of bland titles that have already been used or content that is just plain redundant. Try to find interesting angles that will not only pass muster with the distribution sites but also capture the attention of your readers.

Length is Important - The thing about length is that it can be bad in either direction. If your article is too short, many sites will turn it down and if they don't, readers may assume it doesn't have useful content. If it is too long, it may appear cumbersome to read and many readers will never reach the bottom and find your resource link. A good length should be targeted between 350-750 words. Keep in mind that the standard is 500 words and many sites will require that many words to publish your work.

Create a Brand - This last thing is about as abstract as you're going to find in this book. Creating a brand for you and your business is something that will take time and a lot of articles but that will ultimately result in greater results for the articles you do write. Granted, this strategy is more effective in blogs where readers can be drawn back over and over again, but it still works well in newsletters and article sites.

Create an identity or use your own and maintain a voice or a series of content that will repeatedly draw back readers. Something that will come up time and again in this book as you work on creating content to market your business is consistency and relatability. You need your audience to feel comfortable with you and trust your input. Fail to do this and you'll be fighting for new readers every time you create content.

SEO Guidelines

Keyword Selection and Number - The first thing to consider for SEO is the keywords you will use and how many there should be. Some website owners try to cram multiple keywords into the same article and end up with a jumbled mess. This is a bad route to go. Instead of getting carried away with large volumes of keywords, each article should be focused around a single keyword phrase, usually 2-3 words long. You may add a couple of secondary keywords, but generally speaking, there is no reason to do this as you'll be writing multiple articles and can target those later.

Keyword Density - Keyword density is the number of times your keyword appears in the total word count of the article. For example, if your article was 500 words long and you used a keyword phrase of 3 words 10 times, you would have 30 out of 500 words devoted to that keyword, or 6% of the total. This would be a bit high for most sites. Usually once per 100 words is best or between 3-4%.

Headlines and Subheadings - Keyword placement is just as important as density as some areas of your article are better locations for the phrase than others. Your title should always contain the keyword. This ensures it appears in multiple tags within the code of the page, as well as the title of the browser page and search engine results. Additionally, integrating keywords into the subheadings of your page (if you bold them) will result in better results for those words.

Back Linking Properly - In every resource box you write, you should include a link back to your website. However, do not link to http://www.YourWebsite.com. This is a waste of a link. Rather, use HTML and anchor the link with your keyword. For example, if your keyword was "Station wagon roof racks", your resource link would be:

Learn more about
<a href="http://www.YourWebsite.com">station wagon
roof racks</a> by visiting http://www.YourWebsite.com.

Content Creation Guidelines

Catchy Headlines - How you start an article is a huge factor in how readable it will be. Try to be provocative and interesting without being too controversial and you'll capture more attention. Lists are always good headlines while numbers are easily scanned and capture attention well. Don't just write "Top Roof Rack Options" when you could write "The 10 Best Roof Racks of 2009" instead. There is a major difference in how those two titles will perform.

White Space Use - Blocks of text are hard to read and will quickly push your readers away from the article. You need to utilize white space effectively to break up paragraphs, create rests for the eyes and make a page generally more scan-able. Do this by keeping paragraphs at 5 lines or less, use lots of subheadings and create lists that utilize less space per line.

Scan-ability - Many people will choose to scan through content rather than read it. To accommodate them and still gain their interest, make marker points in your text that will allow them to scan with ease. Bolded subheadings, bulleted lists and key facts in short paragraphs, especially with numbers, are all markers that the eyes will catch on when scanning text, making it easier to keep attention.

Your Bio or Resource Box - How you write your bio is important. However, also keep in mind that it should be unique for every article you write. If you use the same bio over and over again, it is possible that you might start duplicating yourself - something the search engines don't like very much.

Volume of Information - There are two ways to go with this one. You can provide too little information and show that you are uninformed on the subject matter or you can provide too much information and overwhelm readers (and waste valuable material for later articles). Make sure to hit a balance in the middle as often as possible.

What to Write

Knowing what guidelines to stick to is one thing, but what are you supposed to write about. There are dozens if not hundreds of different things that can make good article topics, so what do people actually want to read about?

A good article will do a few things. Here are the ones that you need to be sure of before ever allowing your name to go alongside it:

Show You As an Expert - Your goal is to showcase your knowledge of a topic. So, if you're selling roof racks and you write about how nice a Subaru is for family trips, you're not taking advantage of your knowledge. While this is a good topic that you can use at some point, make sure to write details that other people would not know (without boring them). Throw in the number of people who buy Subarus each year, the volume of people who install roof racks, and other numbers that are interesting. Be an expert and showcase your knowledge in ways that you cannot otherwise do on your website.

Offer Valuable Information - In the same vein, don't just throw random facts at people. Telling someone interested in a roof rack that the upholstery in most Subarus is made from a certain kind of fabric isn't helpful. It seems meandering and will probably lose their interest.

Make Your Business Look Good - Always make yourself look good and your business look better. This is tricky though. Never write about your business in the article or try to sell anything. An article needs to seem impartial to the end. Then, when you have set up a statement such as "a good roof rack is a must have for any family on the go", you can use the bio box to tell your readers that you do in fact sell these amazing devices and that they can find them on your website at http://www.YourSite.com.

Developing a Distribution List

Once you have created a method to write your articles, you need to figure out where to send them. There are a few things to keep in mind when distributing content on the Internet, especially for SEO.

Good Back Links

A good back link needs to come from a trusted, long term website. Don't post content on a site that is new or that has a page rank of less than 3 or 4. These sites provide minimal SEO benefits and in some cases may even hurt you. Look for the higher ranked sites, the bigger databases and wider readership.

Quality Website

You also want a website that readers are going to be willing to visit. There are some sites out there with decent page ranks and an awful interface. This leads to issues where readers are frustrated with finding things, annoyed by bad search technology or upset by poor quality. Don't post on sites that allow poorly written content either - it will come back to hurt you.

Ease of Use

Finally, you want to be sure that your own experience is as easy as possible. Look for sites that are easy to use, quick to upload to and that approve your articles fast. The easier it is for you to use, the more articles you can post - saving you time and making you money.

Top 90 Article Marketing Distribution Sites

The following list is specific sites that allow article posting along with their page ranks in order of usefulness. These sites are all free to use and easy to upload to. If you are interested in a paid service, Article Marketer (www.articlemarketer.com) is a great way to go, distributing your articles to hundreds of sites starting at $34.99 a month. Keep in mind that some of these are industry specific so they may not be quite as useful as the rest. General topic sites have been bolded:

Web Site	Page Rank
www.WebProNews.com	6
www.WebArticles.com	6
www.SelfGrowth.com	6
www.SearchGuild.com	6
www.PowerHomeBiz.com	6
www.EzineArticles.com	6
www.Digital-Women.com	6
www.BusinessKnowHow.com	6
www.BPubs.com	6
www.ArticleDashboard.com	6
www.ArticleCity.com	6
www.Zinos.com	5
www.Web-Source.net	5
www.SideRoad.com	5
www.Marketing-Seek.com	5
www.Jogena.com	5
www.IdeaMarketers.com	5
www.Content-Articles.com	5
www.Constant-Content.com	5

www.BusinessNation.com	5
www.ArticlesFactory.com	5
www.Articles911.com	5
www.ArticleTrader.com	5
www.ArticleAlley.com	5
www.Alumbo.com	5
www.AddMe.com	5
www.Website-Articles.net	4
www.Top7Business.com	4
www.TheAllINeed.com	4
www.SubmitYourNewArticle.com	4
www.SmartAds.info	4
www.SmallBusinessOutpost.com	4
www.Salesopedia.com	4
www.PromotionData.com	4
www.Marcommwise.com	4
www.MainStreetMom.com	4
www.LinkSnoop.com	4
www.HowtoAdvice.com	4
www.Free-Articles-Zone.com	4
www.ExpertArticles.com	4
www.EArticlesOnline.com	4
www.ContentTycoon.com	4
www.ContentDesk.com	4
www.Certificate.net	4
www.BusinessToolChest.com	4
www.BestSellersWorld.com	4
www.BestManagementArticles.com	4
www.AuthorConnection.com	4
www.ArticlesBeyondBetter.com	4
www.ArticlesBase.com	4
www.ArticleSphere.com	4
www.ArticlePros.com	4
www.ArticlePoint.com	4

www.ArticleGarden.com	4
www.ArticleDirect.com	4
www.ArticleCat.com	4
www.ArticleBlast.com	4
www.Article99.com	4
www.ArticleWisdom.com	3
www.VectorCentral.com	3
www.ValuableContent.com	3
www.UltimateProfits.com	3
www.StickyArticle.com	3
www.SmallBizArticles.com	3
www.ReprintArticles.com	3
www.RLRouse.com	3
www.OpportunityUpdate.com	3
www.ISnare.com	3
www.HowItWorks.net	3
www.GuideDawgs.com	3
www.GoArticles.com	3
www.FreeSticky.com	3
www.FreeCoachingArticles.com	3
www.Ezine-Writer.com.au	3
www.Dime-Co.com	3
www.ContentKing.eu	3
www.ConnectionTeam.com	3
www.Articlestop.com	3
www.Articles43.com	3
www.Articleresponder.com	3
www.ArticleWarehouse.com	3
www.ArticleStop.com	3
www.ArticleResponder.com	3
www.ArticleHub.com	3
www.ArticleFinders.com	3
www.ArticleCrazy.com	3
www.Article-Directory.net	3

10 Rules to Live By

The last thing to discuss about Article Marketing and Ezine Marketing is the random little rules and tips that might slip through the cracks if you are not careful. There are some common mistakes that most marketers miss and a few long term benefits that they neglect to take advantage of.

Posting Over Time - Many article marketers will either write or pay someone to write large sums of articles and then post them all at once when they have the time. This is a bad idea for a few reasons. First, the search engines are not going to recognize multiple links from the same site all at once. You get one link and that's all. Second, most of these sites will rise and fall out of the search listings seemingly overnight.

Sure, you get a good listing for a couple days but then, after the article becomes old, it falls away and you lose your valuable link. That's why you want to break up your articles over time. Posting more than 5 articles a week for the same URL is a waste of articles. Make sure to split them up with no more than 2-3 articles every 2-3 days. That way, they will provide the link, and hold that link until you can write more articles and post them in 3 days.

Double Check All Spelling and Grammar - Anything you write out should be carefully checked against a spelling and grammar tool that can ensure that you are on track. This is a vital step because you want to be sure that you don't have any typos or small mistakes that slip through. That will make you look uneducated or sloppy in your work.

Read Your Article Aloud - A second line of defense against poorly written content that I often recommend is to read your articles aloud. You may feel silly doing this, but it's amazing how many more things you'll catch when you hear the article than when you read it silently. Our brains have a nasty habit of skimming over things we compose, missing vital mistakes.

Check Your Titles Against Existing Articles - Go through Google and search for your article titles. Check to see that no other sites or articles have already used that exact title - you don't want to be up against an older, better established article or website than your own.

Keep Things Short - Don't get carried away with anything you write. It's too easy to start going on at length on a topic you know, but if you do, you may risk wasting valuable content that could go into a second article or boring your reader. Shorter is better - 350 words is a good target unless the article directory requires more.

Use Copyscape to Double Check Your Articles - Use the services of Copyscape (www.copyscape.com) to go through and check all of your articles for duplication. You should never plagiarize anything, but even when you make an honest effort not to, it's a good idea to be sure that you don't accidentally copy something from another site.

Read the Submission Guidelines for Each Service - Every article site has a set of guidelines for what they want in your articles. Make sure you read these carefully and know exactly how your articles should look before you submit them. Most of them will be the same (and an article written by the guidelines in this chapter will get you there 99% of the time), but check anyways.

Don't Use Automated Submission - There are dozens of services and software programs out there that promise you automated submission to dozens if not hundreds of article directories for a small fee. These services are dubious most of the time with only a few exceptions (Article Marketer is a good service, though most of its distribution list will not help you in your marketing campaign). Research their services and when all else fails, submit manually.

Research Any Facts You State - Don't start throwing around facts that you vaguely remember or think you know. You can easily start making mistakes and get in trouble, or make yourself look bad if you do. Research anything you say and make sure it is true - better yet, cite a source for that information if you can.

Syndicate Everything - Everything you write should be directly syndicated through a service like Digg, Delicious, or Facebook so that it gets more readers. Do the same thing you do with your blog posts for every article you publish.

CHAPTER 5

List Building via Email Marketing

This form of marketing is one that you may be familiar with, in at least a couple of capacities. Unlike the other marketing formats listed above, this online marketing method is drawn almost directly from offline methods that you are probably already using - building lead lists, marketing to a set list of leads and creating incentive for repeat visits.

List building is a very powerful format that many websites and businesses alike use to create an ongoing, trust building relationship with a customer. They will create an email list or newsletter that customers can opt into. They will then provide valuable information about products, events, or just the niche in general that will create an ongoing relationship with that customer. Eventually, they may return to your website and make a purchase when they find they have a need for a product you sell.

The concept is simple, but execution is very important - especially online where everyone with an email address is faced with upwards of 200-300 spam messages each day. So, for every email list marketer, there are two very important factors that need to be considered above and beyond anything else. First, they need to provide value and incentive in their emails. Second, they need to ensure they follow the rules and don't get flagged as spam, destroying the work they have done.

Building Lists

The concept behind your list building starts with creating valuable content that your readers will want to sign up for. This can be anything from tips related to your niche (car maintenance tips, links to videos or news about cars, etc) to information about your specific business that they might be interested in (upcoming sales, new products, etc). The key though is that you always tell them exactly what you're going to send them. Don't create a list and say it will provide them with valuable information about caring for their Subaru when it will only give them links to your products - this is the very definition of misleading spam and will get you in trouble with your list marketing provider quickly.

Implementation

The first step in putting your list together is finding a service that provides a good autoresponder. An autoresponder is a web service or software that will collect email addresses and user information (usually just a name), and send out emails from a pre-populated list that you have created. Messages can be sent on a set interval of your choosing and you will be able to look at the reader statistics, subscriber numbers, and analytics of your emails as they are read.

The best service in my opinion for this is AWeber. AWeber (www.aweber.com) is at the top of the list for a number of reasons. First of all, their email marketing services provide some of the most accurate numbers and highest delivery rates around. Second, the service is pretty easy to use. Third, it's relatively inexpensive.

For those wondering, you will need to pay a premium for the use of an autoresponder. While some server technologies come with one preinstalled, I don't recommend that you use any of those - they are poorly implemented at best and will give you few of the added benefits that Aweber and similar tools provide. The $19 a month that Aweber costs is well worth a more effective campaign.

Using Aweber

While there are other tool sets out there, the one we're going to focus on is Aweber because of how effective it is in my own campaigns and because of how easy it is to get started with (which is a big bonus for newcomers to online marketing).

In the next section, you will learn what it takes to create your list topics and generate content for them, but for now, let's take a closer look at the tools you'll use to build your list.

Upon visiting Aweber and signing up for an account (you can also sign up for a trial account for $1 to get a feel for it), you will find a bevy of features. Many of these features are for power users - individuals who operate multiple lists across a wide array of domains. You may choose to use those tools in the future, but for now, the odds are that you only need a single list and a single set of emails.

By default, you will be given one list. I recommend you create a new one and name it accordingly. This is the best way to be sure that you have the right kind of setup for that particular list. The best part here is that the Setup Wizard will take you through the creation of your list, asking you to fill in each piece of information needed to create an effective campaign. Here is a rundown of everything it will ask for:

List Name - Choose a good name for your list that will allow you to keep track of it if you decide to create new lists later on.

Description - Add a description for your list.

From Address - The name and email address that subscribers will see when they open your emails.

Subscriber Alerts - When you receive new subscribers or a current one removes themselves from the list, you can set an email address to alert yourself of the changes.

Company Name - The name of your company as it will appear in your messages (used for template emails).

Website URL - The URL of your company as it will appear in your messages (used in template emails).

Logo URL - The logo of your company.

Confirm Message - For this particular section, you need to add your confirmation email subject line, introduction and closing. You can also choose to tell the system what you would like people to see when they confirm their status in your list (after signing up).

Once you have added these particular bits of information, it is time to start creating the messages that will be sent out to your list subscribers. The next section will discuss what content people want to read, how to format it and what you can do to measure the success of your campaign as it proceeds.

What People Want to Read

There are a number of things you can choose to put into each of your emails that will garner attention and warrant the creation of a list. However, the important factor here is that you always keep track of what works and what doesn't work and what will be of the most benefit to your readers. Here are some examples of what they want to read and how to implement lists:

Tutorials - A tutorial sent out in an email is a great way to soften someone up for future sales. Make sure you provide at least a small bit of information that they cannot get anywhere else or that you provide in a special way. Samples include photographic tutorials of car maintenance, tips on how to complete a task related to your products or simply a free chapter from a book you are selling.

Tips and Tricks - Quick tips and tricks given out every few days are a great way to produce interest in your readers and bolster readership in general. Products that utilize multiple tips already are good candidates here as they think they are getting free content, building trust in your knowledge and whetting their appetite for the actual product.

Links, Videos, and Images - Any kind of multimedia, free content, or links that readers may not see elsewhere are going to keep them opening up your emails. Make sure to sprinkle in different kinds here and there to keep your list fresh.

Advice - Offering advice related to the current market for your products is a great way to build trust and develop an ongoing relationship with readers. Having them send in questions is a great way to do this.

Discounts and Sales - If you're an offline business provide sales and discounts only available via email. They gain and you get a loyal customer who will carefully track your newest deals.

Insider Information - If you can show that you learn things faster and provide them before other websites, readers will develop more trust and follow your messages so they can learn more along with you. A great way to do this is with new product announcements, other website launches, links, or news that you get before anyone else.

As you can see from the list above, the essence of each of these is to provide something completely original or better than any other source. That means that you need to understand what your readers want, how they want it delivered and what you can provide that others are not already providing.

How to Format Your Content

The next step in this process is to format your content properly. To start with, never format your content in only HTML or only Text format. It should always be provided in both. Also, make sure that you are careful with image use in your emails. Most email boxes these days will not load images so that they can load faster. Make sure to place text alongside all images in an email that tells readers to turn on their image display so that they can see the entire email.

Next up, make sure your message is not too long. Too many people get carried away with their emails, writing entirely too much content and trying to up sell their readers on how smart they are. Keep in mind that you have as many messages as you want to do this. Aim for compact, useful information that someone would take a minute or two to read. If you write 1000 words they will get bored, almost every time.

Be fresh as well. Don't start every email with the same boring lead-in line about how you have a great tip for them. Make sure they know that you are engaged by personalizing your messages with different bits and pieces of humor, references to messages you wrote in the past, etc. These kinds of bursts of creativity will help you produce more sales per message.

Next, make sure to break up your distribution carefully. Don't just have the messages go out in a big chunk - one every day or two. Break them up effectively with a new message sent out every 4-7 days. This gives them time to stew on your message, doesn't make it seem like you're spamming them every two days, and allows you to create an ongoing narrative they can become interested in. Don't be afraid to send out a broadcast either.

While most messages are stored up in a queue and then sent out automatically, a broadcast is sent out whenever you write it, allowing you much more freedom in what you say. Normally, you'd have to be careful not to say anything time sensitive because you never know when a message will be read. With a broadcast, you know exactly when they'll get it so you can be as specific and personal as you want.

Implementing a List on Your Website

The next step is to find a good location and method to get people signed up for your list. Many marketers recommend a prominent position on the front page. I don't disagree with this, but I do think that putting it directly in front of anything else is a mistake. Rather, I recommend using a sidebar and a nice graphic to illustrate it. Place it as the second or third thing on the left or right sidebar of your page with a form box for visitors to enter their email address and name and a signup button.

Enticing Readership

Make sure that you always tell them exactly what they'll be getting from your messages. This is a big part of getting new readers because they need to feel that they are gaining from the transaction and not the other way around. Tell them they will get "FREE" tips and tutorials or that you will provide ongoing discounts for list members only. This type of language is always enticing. Make sure you remind them that it is optional and they are under zero obligations when they sign up. Another thing many marketers mention is that the information gathered from the forms will not be sold or provided to anyone else. This will help put them at ease about possible spam problems, a big issue for many list builders.

Measuring Success

The most important part of any email marketing campaign is measuring the success of that campaign. Luckily with Aweber, that is relatively easy to do. Upon initial login to your account, you will be able to see exactly how many current subscribers you have as well as how many have recently unsubscribed and how many have failed to confirm their membership.

Next up, make sure that you take a few minutes and look at the statistics section located under Reports on the far right hand side. On the left side of the screen will appear multiple reports that you can gather huge volumes of information from. The first set of reports is for your whole account while the second is for the list you're looking at in particular. Always make sure to look at single list data at a time to get the most accurate data possible.

Here are a few of the more important reports and what they help you learn about your campaign:

Opens Over Time - This statistic will appear as a bar graph that is then broken down by date over a one month period (you can extend to longer periods or different time periods). It will tell you which follow-up emails were opened on which days along with the number of unique views. This ensures you don't think 10 were opened when one person really opened their message three times (meaning only 8 people opened the message).

Clicks Over Time - For each message, you can choose to turn on click tracking. This will allow you to keep an eye on when your subscribers click on the links you provide in the emails you send out. If you have a product link or if you'd just like to see what they are doing after they read your email, this is a good tool.

New Subscribers - This will provide you with breakdowns of new subscribers by day, week, and month, telling you when your subscribers are coming in at the biggest times. It also provides data on those who don't confirm and those that cancel their subscription.

Subscriber Growth - These charts are also provided for daily, weekly and monthly and will show you the percentage growth in the number of subscribers (end over end) from the previous day, week or month.

Subscribe Method - For the most part, this will always be the same with customers filling out the form on your website. However, there are other tools and methods for adding leads that may end up here.

Various Demographics - There is a laundry list of demographics you can use to break down your users by country, state, city, area code, and much more, provided you have that information to work with.

As with Google AdWords, having this information will allow you to see where you are performing better and where improvement can be made to ensure you gather more leads or convert more of those leads.

Avoiding the Spam Issue

The biggest issue that every email marketer needs to consider is spam. You cannot allow your users to hit the spam button or for their filters to start catching your emails and auto-tagging them as spam. Aweber provides detailed information about whether or not your emails are spam or not. They are each scored with a number that measures how likely you are to be tagged as spam. Each infraction will add up and the higher your score is, the more risky your message is. A good score is considered to be below 3.0 with the scale going up to 10.0 (anything after 5.0 is guaranteed spam).

Issues will include usage of words like "Free" or "download", repetition of links, use of too much HTML, or images included along with links. If your emails score higher than a 2 or 3, click on that score and learn how to lower it by reading what was scored and why.

CHAPTER 6

Press Releases

A traditional tool for any marketing campaign is a press release. However, on the Internet, a press release takes on a few different dimensions. While it is distributed through some traditional channels via the media, an online press release is often posted mostly on sites that contain thousands of them. They will appear in Google, syndicate to various article sites, and on occasion be picked up by a media outlet for publication. It is the latter two situations you want to try and coax to happen, which means you need to spend a bit of extra time analyzing and preparing the perfect press release.

How They Work

A press release is a very simple, easily formatted product that will announce a new line of products, an event, or something similar that engages the public with news about your company. They usually follow a fairly set format, ensuring that each news outlet that picks one up knows exactly how they will be set up.

There are a few different ways to distribute and inform the public via a press release as well. There are traditional press releases that may be picked up by print sources - these will appear in online directories where newspapers, magazines, and television networks can sort through them. This type of press release is best for you if you own a local business that might be mentioned in a local media outlet. Online only businesses or companies that are writing press releases for something like a new sale probably shouldn't opt for this though.

The other option is to engage a press release as yet another SEO source. Load it with the right keywords, upload it to the Internet and then allow it to generate valuable back links and new traffic by having it distributed to directories and distribution channels specifically created for press releases. There are dozens of them. You can choose to distribute manually or pay someone to do it for you. The difference between the two is minimal if you have the time for distribution, but if you don't, it can be a very valuable service to have your press release spread around.

The Right Format

Ensuring you have the right format for your press release is important if you want to have it picked up by as many channels as possible. Even if you've written a press release before, you should know that the format has changed greatly in recent years since they went online. Here is a quick breakdown of how your press release should look from start to finish:

Headline

The headline of your press release is a vital part of the whole. It will tell the audience what the content is about while grabbing their attention. It should be written like a newspaper headline, short and to the point without elaborating too much. There should be no hype or references to your products as these will automatically exclude it from consideration from most directories. Make sure to use a standard font as well - such as Times New Roman, Arial or Verdana.

Subtitle

The subtitle usually appears below the headline in italics and adds a few additional details to your headline. Anything with numbers, dates, or program specifics is good to place here as it will elaborate on what you're discussing and create an ongoing narrative in the text.

The Body

The body of the press release can be anywhere between 3 and 5 paragraphs but regardless of length it needs to be written in essentially the same order and format. You need to answer all of the main questions about your press release including "who, what, when, where, and why". Additionally, you should start every press release with the location and the current date.

When you've covered the basics, start to launch into the story. Always maintain a current date and keep the language active and current - the media outlets that pickup press releases want current news - nothing old or out of date. It is recommended that a press release have at least 1 quote, though I often aim for two or three if there is enough length for it. When you do quote someone always add their title and company name following their name to lend credibility to the content as much as possible.

The length of the body should not exceed 800 words and each paragraph should be between 5 and 6 lines at the most. Here is a breakdown of how I like to format my different paragraphs in a 5 paragraph press release:

Headline

Subheader

Paragraph 1 - Introduce the story. Tell the reader what it is you're announcing without using any promotional language.

Paragraph 2 - Introduce the company and the owner. Place your first quote and discuss what the purpose of the story is. If you are releasing a new product, why are you doing so? If you are having an event, what does it support?

Paragraph 3 - List the features and benefits of the product, sale, or event. Tell people what they will receive from your news and why they should care.

Paragraph 4 - List additional supporting data and statistics about your company and the industry. If you are the number 1 car accessories dealer in Syracuse, mention that with the source for that data. Additional quotes are recommended here.

Paragraph 5 - Highlight and outline your company. Mention when you were founded, what you do, and what your website is.

Finish the press release with contact information including your name, organization, phone number, email address and URL.

When complete, all press releases will end with the following symbols to denote the cutting point of the press release - ###. Don't write anything after these signs or it will not be included in your press release.

Search Engine Optimization (SEO)

The final thing to consider in formatting your press releases on the Internet is SEO. While your primary goal may still be to get the press release picked up by multiple media outlets, you still need to create a press release that can be easily searched for and added to multiple databases. This is best done by optimizing for keywords that directly relate to your topic area. Make sure that you keep optimization between 3 and 4 percent at the most as higher numbers can hurt your distribution and make the press release read poorly.

Writing a Press Release

The writing of a press release will be different than anything else you compose for your marketing campaign. It will take a good deal of impartial, careful wording to ensure you don't write anything that is overly biased or promotional. Here are a few tips to keep your press release on track:

Never Compare to Other Products - The biggest goal and the hardest part of any press release is keeping yourself from bragging about anything. This can show up in a number of forms. To start with, you may find yourself comparing to other products or services. Try not to say anything inflammatory or partial - just list what you provide and let the features talk for themselves.

Write with as Few Adjective as Possible - The easiest way to ensure you don't get carried away is to reduce adjectives. Don't say anything like "fast", "easy", "best" or other rather vague, promotional words.   If you stick to the key facts about your products or your business, they will appear much more professional.

Describe Actual Benefits You Have Provided - While most of the press release will focus on the features of your product or business, a good way to list benefits is to describe specific things impartially that your business or products have managed to do. For example, if a pharmaceutical company provided a pill that relieved back pain, they shouldn't say, "will reduce back pain and make life comfortable again". Rather, they should say "clinically proven to reduce back pain in 82% of those who take it".

Use Quotes and Cite Sources Frequently - The more references and sources you can toss into your press release, the more authority you can give to it. This might include quoting yourself, or it might include a quotation from a local newspaper. Always use full titles and dates where applicable.

Read Other Press Releases to Copy Format - A good idea for anyone new to a press release is to review press releases on the Internet to see how they are formatted and written. Read through a few in your own niche to get a good idea of where you are going. This will show you how other companies like yours are writing about themselves while giving multiple perspectives to ensure you see exactly how it should be done.

Add Keywords At the End - While you may start integrating keywords into your press release as you write, I often recommend adding them at the end for this particular type of text. It is too hard to measure the text and its impact while also trying to keep track of how many keywords are in there.

While it is without doubt that your goal is to spend as little as possible, it may be to your benefit to hire an outside firm or writer to produce your press releases. If you only need one or two and you have a lot riding on their distribution, paying a small amount for them to be written properly may be worth your while. However, make sure that you research your options fully and get a good price. Press releases shouldn't cost that much more than a standard article to have written.

Distribution

The final thing you need to consider for your press release is how and where to have it distributed. There are multiple channels through which you can do this, including the free manual sources as well as the large, automated sources.

One thing to keep in mind before distribution is timing. You want to ensure that your press releases go out at the best possible time of the day or week - slow news days are good (you'll have to use your judgment here), as well as early in the day or afternoon when there isn't much on their desks yet. A good time is usually around 5-7am on most weekdays when there are few other stories circulating yet. If someone is looking to fill a slot or hold over some early news, being one of the few available so early will help immensely.

Where to Distribute

The places to distribute a press release will vary depending on your niche and the content of the press release, but here is a good five step process to distributing for free:

Use One or Two Free Distribution Sites - Choose from the list provided below and send your press release to one or two free sites. You want the sites to add your PR to big news engines without having to pay for it (the big ones will charge - this isn't necessary). Sites like PR.com will almost always work well with the free option - don't let them fool you into paying otherwise.

Use the Associated Press - The Associated Press is the big hub for almost all press releases and while they don't pick up or distribute much via the Internet, it isn't impossible to get yourself listed in traditional media by taking this route. Contact your local bureau and submit via fax or email.

Local Newspapers or Media - Again, while it may not turn into something useful, it never hurts to send your press release to local media, especially if they have an online news source that needs content. Hit up their writers and editors directly via email or fax and try to get to know them.

Niche Outlets - There are a wide number of websites, blogs, and magazines on the Internet that serve specific niches. Provide your press release to them and you may get a good boost to your position. Create a list of the top niche sites for your particular industry and always submit content to them.

Publish Your Own Content - You should place all of your press releases on your own website or your blog. This will ensure all regular readers get the news and that you create an ongoing list of archived content on your site - it might be duplicate content, but it actually serves you well if it is well written. Have a press release or news room on your site and file them away there. Then, add things like Digg or Delicious and create social bookmarks back to those PRs for quick exposure.

Free Distribution Sites

http://www.eCommWire.com
http://www.FreePressIndex.com
http://www.Express-Press-Release.com
http://www.Free-News-Release.com
http://www.Free-Press-Release.com
http://www.Free-Press-Release-Center.info
http://www.FreePressRelease.co.cc
http://www.FreePressReleases.co.uk
http://www.i-Newswire.com
http://www.PR9.net
http://www.PR-Inside.com
http://www.PRCompass.com
http://www.PRlog.com
http://www.IndiaPRWire.com

http://www.PR.com
http://www.PRurgent.com
http://www.PRzoom.com
http://www.MediaSyndicate.com
http://www.1888PressRelease.com
http://www.AddPR.com
http://www.BizEurope.com
http://www.PressMethod.com
http://www.PressRelease.com
http://www.PressReleasePoint.com
http://www.TechPRSpider.com
http://www.MyFreePR.com
http://www.NewswireToday.com
http://www.PageRelease.com
http://www.PressAbout.com
http://www.PressBox.co.uk
http://www.PressFlow.co.uk
http://www.TheOpenPress.com

Remember to only use one or two of these sites at a time to minimize the amount of time you spend on distribution and maximize your results without over submitting.

My favorite of the free press release sites are PRlog.com and Free-Press-Release.com. I use both of these sites regularly and have noticed that Google indexes these sites often. If done correctly, your press release can rank high for one of your major keywords.

CHAPTER   7

Viral Marketing

The phrase probably isn't foreign to you - everyone has been talking about viral marketing for the better part of the last 5 years now, but the actual application of this somewhat odd concept is relatively new and while it can be incredibly effective in some situations, it can also be a tremendous waste of time and money if poorly implemented. So, in this chapter, we're going to look at how to integrate various aspects of what Viral Marketing is into the tasks you've already been completing and create a creative new way to market yourself and your business.

Defining Viral Marketing

Viral marketing is the process of providing content or a product that spreads based on its merits and entertainment or creative value rather than through your own marketing tactics. For example, a video produced on YouTube that legions of viewers find funny that also happens to promote a new band will spread not because the band spends money and convinces people to watch their video but because those viewers will send links to friends, share them at work, or put it in their own blog or website.

Viral marketing is the act of finding something that is contagious enough to spread on its merits alone and then setting it loose in the wild. It is the essence of word-of-mouth marketing and when used properly and effectively is the most powerful form of marketing around. On the Internet, it goes beyond one customer telling another that you provide good service though. It can spread throughout the Internet rapidly creating a tidal wave of interest that will drive new traffic and business to your website.

The prevailingly most popular method of creating viral content is via YouTube and similar multimedia sources - however, these websites don't need to be the only way you create such content. Rather, you can build from any online resource and see what comes of it - here are a few that have been successful for many business owners.

The Value of Viral Content

Viral content is valuable for many reasons - here are a few of my favorites and how they integrate well into your already full featured marketing plan:

Social Media Connection - Social media and viral content go hand in hand like nothing else on this list. If you create something that starts to buzz throughout the Internet, you can be assured that social media sites like Facebook or Twitter will spread it faster than any other mediums. It will be passed from user to user, creating a snowball effect of spreading interest - free publicity for your company at the center of it all.

Inbound Links - Next, there is the issue of inbound links. When people like something, they link to it. On blogs, websites and social network profiles around the Internet you will start to gain valuable inbound links to your content because people want to share what you've created.

Long-Term Success - Most people assume that viral content either works or it doesn't, but there is a careful in-between space that you can take advantage of if you know what you're doing. This is where you can create memes and viral content that last because they are timeless. You might create a list entitled "The 50 Best Ways to Accessorize Your Car" and people will always find it interesting, building up new comments and link backs over time.

Encourages Interaction - Not only does adding viral content to a website or blog help to boost your overall visibility, it causes people to raise interest in you and your company and to start interacting with you more often. This might be in the form of comments on a blog you've created or by contacting you with questions about your product. Either way, you're building a brand around your content - something that all Internet businesses should strive for.

What Your Content Needs to Do

For viral content to be successful it needs to do a few things on its own. It cannot just be another article you wrote at 3 am - it needs to be high quality, insightful and well built. Here are a few of the more common factors that you should consider and include in how your content is developed:

Be Well Built - The first thing all viral content needs to be successful is to be quality content. You cannot be successful with poorly written content. It doesn't work very well. The reason people share these things are because they are well structured. If that means you are going to build a list of concepts, make it as long and complete as you can. If it is a video, rack up the production values and be sure it looks good.

Volume of Content - When you deal with written viral content, the larger you make it, the better it is. Of course, quality is still important but if you can ensure quality while making something as long as possible (like our lists mentioned above), you can get a great deal more interest over time, and if you write it so that it is timeless in nature, it'll last for a good long time.

Unique and Interesting - The biggest part of viral content is that it catches people's attention. You need something interesting and unique, or even a little odd to do this. The more different your content is and the more interest it generates, the better it will perform in groups of people who are used to surfing from page to page at light speed every day.

Make People Ask Questions - Think about what you can do to elicit questions and honest curiosity from your readers. This might be in the form of controversy or opinion within your niche or by stirring the pot of intrigue over what your company does. Anything that can capture attention provocatively without damaging your brand is good viral content.

Keep it Accessible - While it is good to think creatively and get ideas that will be original, you need to ensure that your content is as accessible to as many kinds of people as possible. If you're selling car parts and you write a top 10 list entitled "Top 10 Microform Polishing Compounds for Japanese Sports Cars", you're cutting off your audience substantially by being so specific. Think of interesting content that will appeal to large varieties of people and it will spread more easily.

What Can Be Viral

There are a number of different kinds of content that you can craft into viral memes and tidbits. Here are a few of them:

Humor - Anything that people find funny will be spread. They want to make each other laugh and your content, if it does that, will spread fast in the form of videos, jokes, animations, or anything else of humorous value.

Controversy - The essence of controversy is content that not everyone agrees with. Say something bold to grab attention. Be careful with this one though. If you cannot back up your claims or if you say things too bold just to grab your audience, you may find a backlash you cannot control.

Information or Tools They Can Use - Providing value to your users is a highly effective way to grow traffic. Do this by finding resources that they can use and presenting it in as easy to read a format as possible. Links, software, or just plain tips that help people figure things out are always good viral bases.

Lists - A list about anything will grab attention. If it is general, funny, related to your niche or not, people will read it because people are addicted to lists. Just make sure it is original and has some value in it and you'll benefit from adding lists to your blog or website.

Video and Multimedia

There are many ways to utilize multimedia (as you've seen in some examples above) on multimedia sites. However, YouTube is the big one that everyone finds the most useful. Here are some tips on how to use YouTube effectively for Viral Marketing:

Taking Care with Commercial Content

One big thing that all viral marketers need to remember is that you cannot just upload a commercial onto YouTube and expect to make money from it. You need to develop a plan that will allow your video to grab attention and build an audience without openly selling your products.

There are dozens if not hundreds of ways to create content and effectively market it to your readers. You may create videos of special designs you create on your car with polishes or how to accessorize different kinds of cars in goofy ways (17 inch wheels on a 1991 Corsica?) This kind of content doesn't directly market your products, but it shows what you do while building an avid audience. It's an effective way to sell yourself with video content without telling them to "go buy my car accessories".

Of course, you cannot just pretend to be interesting and hope that people will find your videos. You need to come up with content that will grab attention and hold it.

How to Grab Attention on YouTube

There are three primary ways to gather attention to yourself on YouTube, including:

Informational Videos - If you post a video that is informational about your company or your products, people will watch them. You might own a factory and post videos that show how your products are developed and crafted. You may create back story videos about how your company came to exist. Anything that shares general information about your niche will likely be watched.

How To Videos - Any content that will generally create new interest in your company through you showing off your knowledge will always do well on YouTube. You can show people how to craft something, how to use a product you sell, etc. People search for things that start with "How To" constantly, trying to find content that fills a need they have. Provide that content and you'll build your presence on YouTube.

Entertainment - The biggest profile videos on YouTube are going to be those that are funny or entertaining in some format. Such Guerilla marketing tactics may include anything from a short humorous clip with a character to something fun that people will enjoy watching. Consider the case of Blendtec in Orem, Utah. The company creates blenders that are supposed to cut through nearly anything. Their videos show them blending through all sorts of random items and have generated millions of hits as a result.

Once you have created a video that will generate attention, you need to get people to visit your videos and watch them, adding their comments and sharing them with other people. This is a part that many people unfortunately skip over. Here are some tips to help out:

Participate - You need to actually engage in the community on YouTube to get some name recognition and extra traffic. Comment on other videos or join groups and discuss topics in your niche to draw attention back to your videos.

Production Values - If you are creating a video series showing off your factory, don't use a $300 hand held camera that looks awful. Make sure to either write your video so that such a camera makes sense or find a company that can record your video and make it look nice.

Use Keywords Effectively - If you use keywords on YouTube to match up with your content effectively, you will gain more traffic. Unfortunately, there is no search technology that can dissect a video and figure out what it is about, but there are plenty of tools available to help you research your keywords and integrate them. This will help target your hits a bit too. Make sure to title your video correctly, use keywords.

Other Multimedia

There are many multimedia offerings out there as well that can translate to big time success for your website. Just consider the following:

App Creation - A big market in recent years has been the creation and distribution of apps on sites like Facebook or on multimedia enhanced phones like the iPhone. Providing content that is either free or very near free, you can generate interest through games, quizzes, polls, or a software program that does something useful for the person who installs it. In the end, you create one program and it spreads as more people pick it up and you get credit in the form of increased traffic.

Podcasts - Podcasting is very popular because it provides something free and entertaining to people who may be interested in your niche. The key here is to create content that is entertaining in some form or another.

Ebooks and Free Content - Another very popular method of spreading viral messages is via eBooks and high quality free content. Providing a free eBook or content that people will get great use out of with links back to your website can be a tremendous tool in spreading your message and developing a long term strategy for reaching people with content. To do this, make sure to develop something that is unique, 100% original and most of all useful. Upload it to torrent sites, offer it as a free download on your website and send out links on other file sharing services.

Getting Creative - Other Methods

There are many ways to make money through viral marketing, but you need to display a bit of creativity to get it done. You cannot just start throwing out random bits of content that you think people will be interested in. Ask yourself first what people want to see, second what you have to offer that will interest those people, and third how you can promote that thing while getting new traffic to your site. Videos and free content doesn't have to be even the tip of the iceberg if you know how to market yourself effectively.

CHAPTER 8

Blogging

The 800 pound gorilla that everyone knows about and very few people know how to implement properly for their business is the blog - a tool that can boost traffic, build trust, and create an ongoing customer base across the board. There are many different things you're going to be able to do with a well built, frequently updated blog and that makes it one of the premiere tools in your box of tricks.

What Blogs Provide for a Business

A blog is a very valuable tool. Here are a few of the more common things that a blog provides to a business when they start up their own:

New Ways to Communicate with Clients - Clients are the core of any business and good communication with them is vital to being an effective owner. A blog is a great way to communicate, providing ongoing updates on your status, products, and the state of the field. It's also a great way to get down and dirty, answering questions directly from your clients about products, and more.

Personalizing Your Responses - The Internet can be downright impersonal in many ways. It takes much of what we expect from each other out of a business transaction and reduces many people to mistrusting due to the frequency of poor transactions. A blog helps you to identify with your customers, creating a direct line between you as a person and you as a business. When someone cannot meet you and shake your hand this becomes an incredibly important factor to consider.

Funneling Traffic - Your website can always use new ways to get traffic and a blog is a primary way of doing so. It develops and creates an ongoing stream of traffic from search engines and repeat visitors which are all easily sent to your product pages.

Build Trust and Create Prestige as an Expert - Trust and prestige are the next level for someone trying to sell something. A salesman who knows nothing about his or her product is not going to sell all that much in the process. Showcasing yourself as an expert, building a reputation as a trustworthy source of information and building on those two things will help your blog and your business thrive.

You'll Learn More About Yourself and Your Business - Not only will you learn more about yourself as a businessman as you type it out every day for a blog post, you'll learn more about your business. Details about new products, parts of the niche you didn't know before and comments from readers that will guide your research and writing will help you grow into a more knowledgeable owner.

Blogs Are Much Easier and Faster than Traditional Websites to Update - Your main website is going to stay up and running, but if you bypass any news and updates there in favor of a blog, you'll save yourself a tremendous amount of time and energy. A blog is easier to update, faster to maintain, and much better for someone who is in a hurry on a daily basis. Login, write and publish - that's all you need to do.

Relay Information Instantly to Customers - Your customers need information from you that is up to date and relevant. If you have a recall, a sale, or a big new event that is time sensitive, you need them to know about it as fast as possible. A blog allows instant communication - a much easier prospect than almost any other form of communication.

Blogs Are Incredibly Search Engine Friendly when Used Properly - Blogs, when properly integrated into your website and updated regularly will show up extremely high in a search engine in almost every situation. You will find quickly that your blog is a magnet for new traffic. Don't even worry about keywords as much as you do about posting regularly (this is key).

Integrating Other Technology is Easy - As you'll see later, there are numerous other technologies out there that are big on the market right now - from Facebook to Twitter and beyond. These technologies integrate easily into your blog, allowing you to cross over the different sources of traffic and build a larger following in the process.

How to Write Your Own Blog

Now that you've learned a bit more about why your company needs a blog, it's time to start learning how to integrate one into your campaign. The process is actually quite simple - hence its popularity. Here are a few quick tips to get you started.

Choose Your Platform - Decide which platform is best for your blog - the two main options are Blogger (www.blogger.com) and WordPress. Blogger is an online web service operated by Google that you can login to via a web browser. WordPress provides both a similar service at WordPress.com and an installed option, Wordpress.org, where you can upload your own software directly to your server and operate the blog more intensely. This is recommended for anyone that has even a bit of tech savvy or anyone who can utilize the services of a technician or webmaster of some kind.

Setup Your Blog - I'm going to skip over the nitty gritty of signing up for WordPress or Blogger because they're so incredibly easy to get started with. In general, you just need to setup a profile and start writing (they will both take you through entering information about yourself and your blog). If you decide to integrate WordPress into your server, the installation instructions are equally easy and will help you create your blog in about 5-10 minutes. From there, you just need to start writing again.

Figure Out the Theme and Style - Every blog starts out as a blank canvas with a simple theme and a white background. You can leave it like that and start writing or you can customize it. I recommend the latter for a few reasons. First of all, there are more than 300 million blogs on the Internet and they all look similar. If you don't take the time to customize your own and make it look unique, you're throwing away a golden branding opportunity.

Second, you want to be sure that you integrate your personality into the blog as much as possible. This means showing your face, adding some personal details (nothing too specific) and writing a bio for yourself. Steal from your web design for a background or a theme and make sure they link together well with the same color scheme and the same basic font and text layout. If you need to hire a designer for this, wait until you've established a few posts and built a small following. No one will judge you for a basic blog - they will judge you for an empty one.

Start Writing Your First Posts - The next step is to start writing posts that will draw attention and build on your blog's ability to funnel traffic into your website. I recommend you look back at the viral content chapter to learn more about what kind of content people tend to seek out when they are reading blogs.

Additionally though, you want to create an ongoing narrative that builds on your brand's viability. This can be done by writing about your company only passively while reacting as a person rather than a business owner. Write about your life, your view on new products, and any kind of meme that will spread virally.

Advertise Your Blog - You want to get out there, so start advertising your blog. Start with sites like Technorati.com and Pingomatic.com, free services that will syndicate your blog content to feeds automatically whenever you update it. Additionally, ask for link swaps with other blog owners, buy ad space and comment on other blogs. See the section later for more on advertising on other blogs.

Talk with Your Readers - A blog is an interactive platform. You need to interact with your readers to keep traffic up and to continually build on what you've created. This means asking questions in our posts, responding to comments, and writing posts based on what your readers communicate.

Get to Know Other Bloggers and Share Content - You're going to find that whenever you write content, there will be others who want to share it with their readers. Let them. And when you find something that you want to share from another blog, ask for permission to share it yourself. This back and forth creates cross traffic and helps you engage more actively in the blogosphere, getting even more traffic.

Create Memes and Viral Content - If you have not yet, start thinking of topics and working on posts that will have more than just an immediate effect. Things like Top 10, 25, 50, or 100 lists will always translate to solid returns for your business in terms of traffic.

Analyze Your Traffic and Overall Impact - Always look at the statistics on what you're getting done. Use Analytics and see where traffic is coming from, where you're losing traffic and how to make changes. For example, if you see that you are getting 100 hits a day from keywords related to car polish and you only write 1 in 10 posts about polishes, try doubling that rate and see if it boosts your traffic rate. These kinds of tweaks will help you gain more traffic over time as well as immediately.

Marketing Your Blog

Marketing a blog is easier and faster than any other platform because there are so many tools out there already in place to do it with. Sites like Technorati that ping (send messages to validate your connection) your blog constantly and make it easy to get it out there to various RSS feeds and subscribers as well as built in blog search engines are easy to utilize. However, sometimes there are a few tricks you may need to utilize to market your blog faster and more thoroughly. Here are a few tips to get that exposure:

Have a Keyword Glossary - Always build and hold a glossary of good keywords for your blog in a word file somewhere. This will include all keywords that you have seen work well in Analytics as well as those that you have yet to test. Keep track of numbers on what works best.

Optimize your Blog for SEO - This can be done with RSS subscription options, HTML code that is clean (see later in the book for more details), title tags for every page, and a sitemap.

Create Categories with Keywords - Make sure that your categories are keywords that you know will work well for search boosting.

Social Bookmark Links - A great optimization technique is to add links to the top social bookmarking websites like Digg, Reddit, Delicious, and Facebook at the end of each blog post where users can submit them quick and easily.

Have a Google Webmaster Account - Submit your sitemap automatically to Google through http://www.Google.com/webmaster where you can see all of your site stats as well.

Find Top Blogs - Find the top blogs in your category and link to them from your blog roll and link list to effectively create an ongoing traffic flow.

Submit to Directories - You can appear in blog directories like Technorati as well as normal ones like Yahoo!, BOTW and DMOZ.

Hit Up Forums and Ask for Reviews - Ask people in forums to comment on your blog and generate additional content about how you are writing and what can be done better (if anything).

Post Often - The biggest thing you can do is to write as much as possible. News blogs need to post at least 2 or 3 times a day while general info blogs (which most businesses run) should be updated every day or two. If you cannot do it yourself have someone else in your company create a login and start posting as well.

Respond to All Comments - Whenever you get a comment, respond to it and build from it. Make mentions of specific comments in posts as well to make your readers know you are engaged.

Cite Sources - Cite other blogs or websites with as many links as possible. Use other blog names as well. They will see back links and mentions and possibly mention you back.

If you get enough information written in your blog, get a press or media badge and start going to related events in your niche. You can then blog about those events.

Advertising on Other Blogs

While most of this chapter focuses on getting interest in your blog so that you can funnel traffic over to your website, there is something to be said for advertising your website or your blog on other blogs. Traffic generation on a blog is about as easy as it comes and if you find a good blog in your niche with a ton of readership that is willing to sell ad space to you, you should take advantage of it.

What Makes This Different from PPC?

While PPC is something that works directly through search engines, you already know the readership of a blog - it's easy to figure it out based on the posts and topics. So, you know what you're paying for when you post an ad there. Additionally, you can opt for larger banner ads as well as pay per impression setups that will allow you to pay for exposure rather than just clicks.

How Much does it Cost?

One of the best things about blog advertising is that you don't necessarily need to pay for it. Let me explain this a little bit. First off, if you want a big banner ad on a highly read blog's front page, you'll probably pay. However, when you can start bypassing the cost of a blog is when you start swapping exposure or offering free content in exchange for a plug. Here's what I mean:

Swapping - Swapping is good because you and the other blog can both benefit from each other's traffic without either of you paying all that much for it. Some blogs will do this in the form of link roll swaps while others will write reviews or pages of content about their swap partner. However you do it, make sure it is even and that both sides are aware of the exposure that they are giving.

Free Content - One of my favorite ways to get exposure without paying anything is to offer my services as a 'guest blogger' on a popular site. You'd be surprised how often this will work. Major blogs in various niches have been happy to allow me to write up a short post or review of a product or service in the niche with a short plug at the end mentioning the website I'm working on. Always approach these bloggers from a professional email address and make sure they know you are not interested in a straight plug. Actually offer them valuable, original content (no reprints), that they can use for a post in exchange for a short blurb about your product or service. Not only is it good exposure, it's an easy way to generate free back links.

CHAPTER 9

Social Media

Whereas blogging was the major platform of choice for so many Internet marketers for so long, recent trends have shifted towards the Social Media platforms that have become so popular - sites like Facebook and Twitter. These sites have made it easier than ever to interact with people on levels unheard of before and for marketers they are demographic dreams, providing instant access to set numbers of individuals that have hashed out their interests, their goals and their needs all in one easy to reach database. For any Internet marketer, mastery of these tools is almost necessary to be effective in the current market.

Facebook and Social Networking

Social networks are a huge part of the online landscape with an estimated $1.3 billion spent on them in 2009 alone. There are a number of ways that you can market your business using these tools, either spending money or for free. Before diving into all those different methods, let's take a closer look at what the social networks are and how you should be using them.

MySpace.com started it all off with the first giant social network on the Internet (it wasn't the first in general, just the first big one). However, Facebook.com took it to new heights by creating a highly accessible, easy to use format that was perfectly suited for business owners as well as people looking to socialize.

Each service provides basically the same thing - a way to post a profile and update friends or fans about your life. You can friend people from around the globe, update content from your computer or your phone and create new relationships instantly. As you can imagine, this makes it a highly useful resource for business owners looking for a way to build their lead bases and create new avenues for revenue.

There are a number of ways that you're going to use these sites for marketing purposes. You can choose to either post simple ads on the pages or to actually create profiles and market to the people who use them every day. Either way, you'll need to know how the sites work, what is expected of you in terms of behavior and how to blend it all together into a viable marketing strategy.

Using Facebook

While MySpace is still a big resource that has a lot of users (over 200 million), Facebook has more active users on a daily basis and a much greater foundation for business owners. You'll find that you can easily integrate your business profile into a Facebook Page or create ads that hit up specific demographics with ease.

Signing Up and Using Facebook

Signing up for Facebook is incredibly easy. All you need to do is have a few good details about yourself ready to enter into the profile. I generally recommend that you start out with a profile about yourself and then upgrade to working on your business once you have a personal profile in place. Additionally, you should create a specific email address only for Facebook interactions. If you have a business email that you use more casually, that works as well but you don't want a customer service inbox or a personal inbox cluttered with friend requests and messages.

Sign Up - Sign up for Facebook and enter your personal information into the boxes that it provides. This includes your full name, company information, personal details that you may want to share (I'd leave this blank for now), etc.

Add Friends - Next, you can add friends directly from your instant messaging and email accounts. Just enter your login information and Facebook will sort through everything to find people that can be added.

Affiliations - Next, add any affiliations you have. You will be added to networks according to what you put here. People in networks with each other can view profiles of each other without making them friends. This doesn't mean a whole lot to you, but you should probably enter your college, high school, and any local groups you may want to include. You will also need to enter your hometown - make sure to be as specific as possible, especially if you are an offline business.

Your Profile

Once you've signed up, your profile will be ready to use. You will either be able to log directly in and start looking at friends or you can start editing parts of your profile. I recommend you do the latter so that we can start focusing on marketing methods you're going to use.

Profile Picture - Choose a good, full head and shoulders image of yourself for the profile picture. It should be professional, but display you in your natural habitat - either working or doing something you enjoy. Make sure you're smiling.

Basic Profile Information - The basic profile information tab includes your hometown, sex, birthday, political, and religious views. Make sure that you leave the potentially polarizing information blank unless it is helpful to your particular business. (e.g. Christianity if you sell Bibles).

Contact - Enter you contact methods here to give your friends as many options as possible to reach you. I recommend entering personal contact information here that you are comfortable sharing, then saving your business contact information for the Page you will soon create.

Relationships and Personal - This data is entirely up to you. Relationships is an option that teenagers and college students get a kick out of but that you can choose to ignore if you'd rather not broadcast that information to the world. Personal information includes details about what you enjoy, what your favorite books and movies are, what websites you like, what quotes you'd like to share with your friends, etc. Make sure to fill out all of these sections at least once and don't share anything you wouldn't want a business associate seeing.

Education and Work - For education and work, you will enter where you went to school and where you have worked. This should be pretty straightforward; just don't enter any past jobs you had that conflict with your current business.

Layout - This is an option to change how your page looks - I wouldn't bother with this if I were you. Facebook is pretty standardized and moving too much around can just confuse new friends and anyone looking to learn more about you as a person.

There are numerous other things you can do with your Facebook profile, including adding applications and various other fun little tidbits to the page. I will not delve into that aspect of the service, but keep in mind that if you think there is something that would be fun to do, there is probably an option out there to make it happen. Just search for it in Google or in the Facebook Applications database.

Facebook for Your Business

Now that you know a little bit more about Facebook, let's take a look at how Facebook integrates into your business more directly. The main profile you set up is going to be for you, the business owner. You may or may not choose to actually use it, but it is a good idea to have it up and running to personalize the business page you are about to create.

Pages on the other hand are different from Profiles - they are a special subset of Facebook that allows businesses, celebrities and bands to build a following and communicate directly with them as a business rather than as the owner or an employee of that business. You'll find them under the advertising section, located at the bottom of any Facebook page.

In addition to Pages, Facebook allows you to integrate advertising directly into your profile, with both PPC and PPI (pay per impression) advertising, both of which allow for highly targeted, demographic rich integration. There are also a couple of other fun little things you can do, such as running a poll.

Your Facebook Page

To create a Facebook page, click on "Create a Page" under the "Sign up" button on the homepage. You will find an option there to create different types of Pages. Choose the one for local businesses (even if you are not local). Additionally, you can choose to create a page for a brand, product or organization, or for an artist, band or public figure. The latter will probably never be of use to you, but you may find that you have a brand name or product that works well in a Facebook environment.

The page you create here will be accessible directly through your personal account, but it will not be linked to that account. So, your friends will not know you are running the business page and your fans on the business page will not be able to view your personal page (unless you choose to let them).

Unlike when you create a profile, a Facebook Page is completely blank when you set it up. There is no data or links on it other than your company's name, so you're going to need to go through and add some content.

Page Photo - You should choose at least one photo to upload - preferably a logo or store front that will show who you are without people needing to read any text. Additionally, I recommend uploading at least five or six additional photos to an album, much in the same way you did for your Local Search profiles. This will create an additional set of content that your fans can look through and learn more about you with.

Mini-feed - This part of the page will display only the content that you want it to - including actions taken by administrators of the page or fans of your business.

Information - This section on your page will include whatever details about your business you want to share. I like to tell businesses to be careful here. There are a few reasons for this. First off, you want to be sure you don't get carried away and have a giant wall of text. Second, you want to be sure that you have enough details that they know what you do. If someone reaches your business page, sees your nice logo and a lot of activity but has no idea who you are or what you do, what good is the page? Add products, a list of services you provide, what you provide that is unique, and your goal of being on Facebook (to meet fun new people in your community). Keep this from being a sales pitch if at all possible - that will only scare most people away from it.

Discussion Board - All of the Pages that you can create in Facebook have an option for the Discussion Board which allows you to talk directly with your fans about questions they may have about you service or products. Pre-populate the Discussion board with as many questions as you can think of beforehand to show people you are involved and whenever someone asks a question, be sure to answer it within 2 days - the last thing you want is interested parties walking away because it's taking you too long to reply.

Fans - The fans box is a bit misleading because you don't necessarily have fans - just customers. However, the wording is taken from the brands and artist Pages that use that terminology. Either way, this is the place where people can sign up to follow your comings and goings on Facebook. You cannot request fans here though - you must actually go out and try to draw them to you.

Videos and Notes - You can post all sorts of different things to your profile for people to peruse. Remember how I mentioned how great viral content is on Facebook? This is where you share it. Post videos you create for YouTube, links to viral posts you do on your blogs or notes that you want to share with fans. This is a great way to spread new deals and sales you're having as well.

Events - The events feature is a great way to invite your fans to come to your store or website and partake in a special event you're having - this can include a sale, a promotion, or an actual event you're holding to draw out new customers. Make sure to be detailed about the event with pictures, addresses, and maps as needed.

Utilizing Your Page

Once you have your page set up, you need to start marketing it in a way that will draw customers. This can be done in any number of ways - primarily, you need to be sure you don't violate the Facebook Terms of Service (I recommend you read them thoroughly before starting any projects).

Next, you need to build trust from your fans. This is best done through communication. Send notes, write on their walls and comment on their photos. Make sure to engage them on your own wall and respond to all inquiries or comments on the Discussion Board. When you do this, they will pay closer attention to your profile so that when you do something that will create business, they will pay attention.

Creativity is the biggest goal here. You need to stand out. Use the tactics you learned in the chapter on Viral Marketing to draw attention to your profile and then funnel that traffic off to your main website or store front.

Advertising on Facebook

If you decide you would like to move beyond the social aspects of Facebook (i.e. the free parts) you can start injecting some advertising money into the site and get your links posted to a select audience all over the world. With nearly 200 million users on Facebook and each of them providing detailed locations, ages, sexes, and interests, it's not that hard to get your ads shown to the exact people you want.

The Facebook Advertising section is located at http://www.facebook.com/advertising and permits you to target specific actions, post ads and then to track and optimize your ads and get the most out of them.

When you click on "Create an Ad" you will be taken to a design page where you put your ad together. The ads on Facebook are similar to the ones you used in Google AdWords. You are given 25 characters for titles, 135 characters for the body and a space for your URL. You can also choose to add an image, which is a big plus here. I recommend doing this, especially if you are doing pay per impression ads as you want people to see it as much as possible. I won't go over how to write your ad again as there is sufficient content earlier in the book to help you do that, but you should spend a bit of time composing a good ad before proceeding.

Targeting Your Ad

Next up, you can target your ad to a specific audience using the demographic tools that Facebook offers. You will be able to narrow in on an audience with the following specific groups:

Location - Choose by country, state, or city to narrow in on your target consumer.

Age - From 13 to 64 you are given leeway here to choose what ages you want seeing your ad. There are specific rules about ads that go out to people under 18 though, so be careful there.

Sex - Male or female. You can choose both as well.

Keywords - You can choose a list of keywords that your ad will target. Unlike Google, these will match to keywords already on the pages of the profiles you target.

Education - Choose between College Grads, In College, or In High School. You can also choose to target them all.

Workplaces - You can target people who work for specific companies as well. This might be useful if you have a specific product you'd like to sell to someone who works for another company.

Relationship - This may or may not affect you. Select all of them if you don't care or delineate between which ones are best.

Languages - You can also choose which languages to appear in.

Once you have entered the data for the different demographics you'd like to target, Facebook will give you an estimate of how many people are eligible to see your ad. For example, if you leave it on the default - anywhere in the United States over 18 years of age - there would be around 54 million people.

Social Actions

By default, your ad will be very similar in style (though more highly targeted) to Google. The links will provide direct access for those who see the ads to go to your website or blog and then purchase products from there. However, you may also choose to use your Facebook Ad to target a social action. Social Actions are ways to get people to do something on Facebook and might include:

- ❖ Visiting Your Business Page
- ❖ Taking a Poll
- ❖ Using or Installing a Specific App
- ❖ Promoting Other Facebook Elements

By setting up a Social Action, you can directly guide how they interact with you on Facebook, something that no other social media site offers quite as well.

Budgeting Your Ads

Budgeting in Facebook is similar to how it works in AdWords. You need to choose a total budget per day, then a maximum bid price per click. Each demographic has a different minimum bid price, so you'll be stuck with what that demographic demands rather than what the keywords demand (as is the case with Google). You can also choose to pay per 1,000 views. If you feel the exposure is enough on its own, this is a way to get much more views with slightly less payment (usually between $0.25 and $1 per 1,000 views).

Branding Your Business with Facebook

So far, we've discussed how Facebook operates, how to create an ongoing relationship with friends and how to place ads on the service. However, to be truly effective, you need to ensure your focus is on how you brand your business. Here are a few tips for controlling your branding strategy on the site:

Image Use - Don't just post random images from your store. Post images of your employees having fun, customers interacting, new products being displayed prominently, etc. Make people want to be a part of the experience.

Managing Friend Lists - Make sure that you friends list doesn't get out of control and that you are able to maintain those that you friend. Becoming friends with celebrities is a waste of time for that reason - they won't interact with you and they only clutter your friend list. Be sure you can respond and stay involved at all times.

Creating New Content - Use Facebook at least once a day. Add something new regularly to ensure you remain on people's newsfeeds and they constantly see your face or your business. Don't overdo it though as you don't want people to think you're spending too much time on there.

Developing Your Personality - Make sure people know who you are as a person, not just what you sell. Provide them with solid reasons to read what you have to say and to visit the links you provide.

Involvement - Remain involved, contact friends, write on the discussion board, and provide good reasons for your friends to be interested in you as a person.

When used properly, the tools that Facebook provides will integrate seamlessly into your business's brand and allow you to effectively control what people think of you and how they interact with your services and products.

Twitter

Twitter (www.twitter.com) is the next big tool in the social media landscape, providing a large deal of new options for businesses that are interested in spreading their reach online into multiple new arenas. Let's take a quick look at what Twitter is and how it works, then how you can utilize it effectively to build your marketing plan:

What Twitter Is and Does

The first thing to understand about Twitter is what it is and how it works. The essence of the site is that you can create and publish 140 character long messages that users can read from anywhere in the world via computer, phone, or other electronic device. You can also maintain contact and direct various bits and pieces of information between yourself and your followers with ease, saving you vast amounts of time in the process and making for a highly interactive means of communication.

It is an incredibly easy to use format that has been growing exponentially since it first hit big in 2007 and as you'll soon see there are countless ways to leverage the technology present in Twitter to big effect. Your goal will be to gather followers, individuals who sign up to keep track of your posts. You will also be able to follow other Twitter profiles, something that will allow you to track other experts in your field as well as friends and family you may be interested in talking to.

What Some Use Twitter For

Twitter may seem incredibly simple at first glance, but people are using it for a wide variety of different goals including:

- ❖ Customer Service Contact
- ❖ Rebranding to a New Audience
- ❖ Following People Who Are Experts So You Can Draw On Them
- ❖ Building a Brand and Ongoing Narrative for Your Business
- ❖ Building New Paths for Business Success
- ❖ Adding a Community to Your Business that Will Help it Grow

We'll take a closer look at how these different uses allow you to leverage Twitter into a tool for expanded uses in your business, much the same way as Facebook.

The Twitter Profile

Signing up for Twitter takes about 2 minutes. You create a URL username, add any friends or contacts you may have in your contact lists, and then start tweeting. However, for a business owner, it is very important that you master how your profile looks before you start writing about anything for your business. Here are some important tips for how to optimize your profile for Twitter to ensure it is effective in portraying your brand:

The Background

Your profile background is a very important part of how your Twitter profile will look. To start with, you will need to ensure that you don't waste any space on a business profile. By default, Twitter's profiles are filled with wasted space. They contain large chunks of space that is just being filled with an empty image. So, instead of leaving it that way, you should consider using a premade background, provided by a top designer or to go into Photoshop and craft your own image.

The basic outline of a Twitter profile is only 1900x650 and 800Kb (maximum) and can be filled with anything you want. Since the update, only 41-110 pixels are viewable on both sides depending on the screen size. I recommend you focus only on the space to the left of your Tweets. This will allow you to put a larger picture of yourself, a logo for your business and if you like, additional text and contact information. If you look at the Mashable profile, creator Pete Cashmore has added an additional photo of himself along with contact information along the left side of his profile page.

Bio Line

The bio line is the next thing you should take a close look at. The bio is only slightly longer than the standard 140 character tweets that you can do in Twitter so you're going to find that it is very similar in many ways. However, you need to optimize how it appears and not waste any of the text space you are given. Here are two examples of how a good bio should look:

Example 1 - I'm a car lover who likes to sell the same parts and items that have made me so happy in my career.

Example 2 - Car lover, finisher and detailer, I've been

*working on classic, muscle, and factory fresh cars for my
entire career, both as a hobby and as my business.*

The difference here should be evident - the former is flat
and lacking in detail while the latter showcases everything
you need from your bio line - info about you along with
details about how it integrates into your feed and your
career.

Profile Picture

Next up, you need to find a good profile picture. For a
business profile, this can be done either as a logo or
storefront or as an upfront picture of you. I recommend the
latter because the best way to leverage a Twitter profile is
to write from your own perspective, not that of your
business. Make sure that you find something with good
lighting, an inviting smile, and you as you truly are - don't
gloss it up or try to make yourself look better. Just be you.

Your Follower: Following Ratio

The last thing to think about is how many followers you
have versus how many following you have. When other
people see a profile, if they see you are following a large
number of people but very few are following you, they will
assume you are spamming people. For example, if you
follow 8,000 people and only have 32 followers, you
probably are trying to pester people too much. Try to keep
the number close, both to keep this connotation from
popping up and to reassure people that you are available at
all times and will not ignore them if they follow you.

Balancing Your Tweets

On Twitter, there are many different types of tweets that
you can publish. How those tweets appear will have a
tremendous impact on what potential followers think of

you, so you want to have a good balance to them - in a way that will showcase your expertise without sacrificing your

personalization. We'll discuss the different types later, but know that @responds (tweets written directly at a particular person), retweets, and questions should be balanced effectively.

Talking on Twitter

Next up, you need to learn how people talk on Twitter and how to effectively blend into that environment. Imagine having to say everything you need to about your business in 140 characters. Now imagine doing it over and over again every day. It will be hard the first time and harder still the next and the next. So, you need to learn how to effectively use brevity in your writing, getting to the point, writing just sections of what you have to say and cutting out anything unnecessary.

You also need to be sure that you always provide some value in what you are saying - being up front is one thing, but just plain skipping over valuable content is not going to be any use to your followers - they will think you are wasting their time. Here are some of the tweet types and how they should be used:

The @Respond

The first type of tweet is the @respond. This Tweet is directed at a particular user and can be used to answer a question, comment on a tweet, or carry on a conversation. Since one of the most important things you can do on Twitter is to carry on conversations, you should maintain the use of this as much as possible without sacrificing the integrity of your timeline with a ton of them that don't affect most of your followers. Here are some instances you can use them in:

Questions - When someone posts a question you know how to answer, you can show them you're involved by answering the question while also showing other readers that you know what you're talking about. Try not to do this too much every day or you'll push too far and annoy your followers.

Event Discussions - Talking about things that are big deals such as a recent conference or nearby events can be effective with the @ respond, allowing you to carry on conversations with other users about what is happening.

Strategies and Tips - Add to a strategy, share it with other followers or ask a question to someone about something they have posted with the "@" symbol.

Status Updates

Another type of Tweet that you will get a great deal of use out of is the Status Update. The Status Update is as simple as it gets - you telling your followers what you are doing. However, always remember to include details about how that information affects them and what you are thinking about. Additionally, minimize how many times a day you use this as you don't want to bore people with what you're doing all day.

Opinions

As an expert in a field and a business owner, having an opinion means that you can get a great deal of weight into what you say in a tweet. People will read them because they are probably actively waiting for someone with knowledge to tell them about a new product or a new opportunity out there. It will also allow you to draw people back to your website more easily by creating ongoing and honest lists of opinions about products and services related to your niche.

Jokes and Entertainment

One of the biggest and most successful things you can put into any Twitter feed is something entertaining. It might be a link to a funny video or just a joke that you think other people would enjoy reading. Either way, adding it to your feed will gain you attention - just be careful not to overdo it - people still want some value in their content as well.

Links

Linking to outside websites is always a good idea as well. This can be done in a couple of different ways. You can either link to content you have written, such as the stuff that you post on your blog, or you can link to other pages you think are valuable to the type of follower you have - mainly references or highly useful resources of some sort.

Re-tweets

Another form of tweeting that is very popular is the re-tweet. This is basically a forward of a message one of the people you are following posted. For example, if someone you follow posted a message that had a good link in it that you think others on your list would enjoy, you can re-tweet it as follows:

RT @username MESSAGE

As you can see, the RT just says that you copied and pasted someone else's message, then you mention whose message you copied. It's a way to give credit where it's due.

Gaining Followers

The crux of Twitter is to find and hold followers - the people who choose to add your feed to their list and keep track of everything you post. You need to give them a reason to want to follow you and then ensure they never have a reason to stop following you. Here are a few quick ways to find and acquire followers for your feed:

On a Blog - When you have a blog, you have a built in audience. Translate that audience to Twitter by telling them to follow you from your blog. Have a Twitter feed button on your web page that they can easily access and they'll likely join in.

With Widgets - Widgets are useful to show people on a blog or a social media profile like Facebook what you are posting on your Twitter feed. It will also engage them to follow you and keep track of those posts.

Conversation - Engage in conversations and you'll gain more followers. Not only will you make the person you talk with more interested, the @responds you post will show up in your feed as well as their feed and draw more interest to your profile.

Following Other People - While you don't want to follow too many people (lest your ratio gets too skewed and people start avoiding your profile), you do want to follow some people, largely experts in your field. I like to tell people to follow 50 people at a time more than what you have following you. This will allow you to get new followers in small bursts without skewing your ratios. Always look for experts and similar niche writers that you can share content with and get new followers through.

Giving Things Away - The single easiest way to get someone to follow you on Twitter is to give them something they can use, especially if it is free. If you're a brick and mortar business, do this in the form of discounts or coupon codes. If you're a web business, have a contest of some kind. Either way, if you give something away, people will follow you just to keep up with your freebies.

Following Up - Always follow up on messages you get. If someone Direct Messages you or sends a @respond to a message you post, reply. It will always help you boost your visibility.

Creating Viral Tweets - This isn't as easy as it sounds. You need to find something that will spread via re-tweets quickly and that means knowing what people will be interested in. Find good links, funny jokes, or useful insights and hopefully you'll get lucky.

Brand Building

The last thing I want to talk about with Twitter is how you're going to start leveraging your business's presence there into income, including how it will work when you start branding yourself more intensely in a digital space where you have constant input from outside sources.

Fitting In

This isn't something many other people will discuss when it comes to things like Twitter, but the truth of the matter is that the number one thing I see go wrong for many companies that take to Twitter or Facebook or any other social media space for that matter is that they don't make the effort necessary to fit into their surroundings more readily. This doesn't mean understanding the Internet any better or talking like a 22 year old male (don't do that).

What it means is seeing these tools as community driven spaces rather than a big mesh of possible customers. You need to be engaged and you need to foster conversation - these are the two biggest things you can do to be successful and fit in properly. Just having a Twitter profile doesn't make you high tech. You need to use it properly.

Creating and Protecting Your Message

As a business, you have a message - whether it is a carefully crafted message you paid a marketing guru multiple figures to come up with or it's just a simple mission statement that you want to make sure conveys how you do business. That message exists and you should make sure it is presented carefully to your Twitter followers. Include it in your posts (if you're a funny guy, be funny - if you provide advice, be sage), in your profile's images and in how you hold conversations.

Once you've created that message, protect it. Don't suggest people try out other products because you're not sure your newest is going to cut it for what they need. Don't tell them what you really think about something. You can be sincere without sacrificing the hard work you did to build your brand. Don't send links out that are not representative of your brand. Don't promote things you do not believe in. Don't write content that you will regret later. Be strict with yourself and protect what people see in you.

As an example, take a look at the Comcast Twitter feed at http://twitter.com/comcastcares. This page was built in response to the constant barrage of angry tweets against Comcast that fill so many timelines. Instead of just posting a basic company profile, Comcast put up a highly skilled customer service representative and then had them engage the audience in a way that showcases how the company has grown from its customer service impaired days.

They now have more than 46,000 followers and have been featured in the New York Times and Wall Street Journal as companies that are rebranding successfully with the use of technology. You may not need to rebrand like this, but you will need to spend a bit of time considering how you can present your company in a way that will positively engage your customer base.

Leveraging Twitter Exposure into Income

The big goal with Twitter and all of the techniques in this book is to make money and with Twitter especially it might seem complicated to pull that off. So, let's take a look at some of the ways that people are leveraging the collection of followers they've built into income for their business.

Leading Advice - This is a tricky one, but if you are selling products on the Internet, it will work well when done properly. To provide leading advice, you need three or four quick Tweets in a row throughout the course of a day. The first might introduce the idea of a product. The second would tell people you like the product. The third will tell them that you like it so much you want to write a review or recommend it. The fourth will do that. Here is a timeline example:

Got new Bertha Driver today - can't wait to hit the range and test it out.

Bertha was a major hit - drove at least three to the end of the range - 300+ yards.

Going to do a full write up of Bertha today - can't wait to share how great this new driver is.

Review of Bertha is up on my blog - check it out at: http://tinyurl.com/23423kj

As you can see, this sequence builds on a basic stream of advice that ends with you sending your followers to a review of a product you might sell. It's a great way to prep people before trying to sell them on something - this works just as well for in store promotions and brick and mortar products.

In Store Promotions and Discounts - This method is much easier to do. You just tell people that you have a promotion or discount coming up that is only for Twitter followers. It provides incentive to read your feed and gives them a reason to come into your store and builds on existing business. Make sure you always provide an added bonus for posting these. Don't just say "we have new skis in this month". Tell people they're on sale too.

Changing Your Business - There are some measures that have been taken by other businesses that have quite literally changed how those businesses operate. One example is a Texas coffee shop owner who utilized Twitter to start allowing his customers to order food and drinks from their computers.

He put in a drive through window and they could come through after ordering on Twitter. It kept his feed active, nearly doubled his business and developed into a local business success story. This might not apply to your own business, but using Twitter in such creative ways will not only be effective in many cases, it will engage a youth-base that is always hungry for fun new ways to use technology.

Direct Marketing - The simplest way to talk to people on Twitter about your products is simply to try and sell them something straight up. Post links, tell them about products, or sell them on a sale you're having. This needs to be done carefully but if you have a strong brand and provide enough valuable advice or entertaining posts throughout your feed that aren't promotional, they'll be much more willing to follow your lead when you try to sell them something.

CHAPTER   10

10 Organic Search Engine Optimization (SEO) Tips

Throughout this book we've discussed everything you could possibly need to create a top notch marketing plan for your business on the Internet. From paying for ads to creating detailed methods to reach new audiences across multiple platforms, your campaign has been a wide spread net to build on what you already have in your business. Amongst all of that, the primary goal is always to build a long term search engine optimization plan that will allow you to reach more people organically, without spending any money. To go toward that goal even more, here are 10 top tips to help in the optimization of your website for free, organic listings for your website with select keywords in your niche.

Choosing Keywords

I won't delve too deeply into keyword research because, for the most part, you're going to find that keyword research for your website is the same as it was for your PPC advertising campaign. However, one thing to keep in mind is that you now need to worry more about the keywords that people will search for regardless of whether they are buying or not. Additionally, you want to create multiple sets of keywords including ones for:

- ❖ Front page content
- ❖ Navigation structure
- ❖ Meta tags
- ❖ Articles and additional content

The landing page or front page is the most important of any of this content, but you're going to need to focus more intently on the other pages in your website.

Domain Name and URL Optimization

The domain name you choose and use for your website doesn't have quite the same impact as it once did on your SEO efforts, but it is important that you spend a little bit of time considering what you purchase. Most businesses will attempt to get the URL that matches the name of their company. Others will have a branded strategy where the URL doesn't reflect their niche at all but they will be able to work with the brand they have developed in the past.

For everyone else, it is important that you spend a bit of time researching and learning exactly what you are getting with your website's domain name. Check out the current traffic numbers, how effective they might be and how easy the domain name is to type into a browser. You may decide to purchase more than one domain name if you find several useful URLs.

Additionally, the URLs that you use should all be optimized for SEO. This means that your file names and folders should be effective in SEO concerns. Here is an example:

http://www.YOURSITE.com/keyword/keyword.html

While this may not have a profound impact, it helps the search engines with internal filing and later crawling when the keywords are used heavily in the text in this manner.

META Tags

There are two main META tags present in every web page that need to be filled out for SEO purposes. Each of these META tags will be used by the search engine spider for processing and include:

KEYWORDS - the META KEYWORDS tag is used to enter as many keywords as you can or need to that may not appear on your page. It is not supposed to be stuffed with keywords that you have already used or misspellings of words (recently, Google started to penalize this). Any words that you research and do not find good use for should go into this list.

DESCRIPTION - the META DESCRIPTION is slightly more important than the KEYWORDS tag because it is used to describe the website to the search engines and is often used as the text that appears in search results for visitors. Make sure to use at least your main two keywords and aim to keep it under 160 characters.

The META tags need to be different for every page on your website to be effective, so make sure you don't copy and paste them.

Titles

The titles of each page are about as important as the meta tags. Like your URLs, the titles will be picked up in the HTML by search spiders and will be given special weight as keywords. I recommend using the title of the specific page first, then a short description, then the title of the company. For example, a good syntax would be:

Polishes and Waxes | Top Car Polishes and Waxes for all Makes and Models | CarPolishes.com

This Title tag would fill up just about all the text allowed atop a browser window while ensuring that the primary keywords for the page are shown before anything else.

Navigation Structure

The structure you use in your website will be important as well for SEO. This comes about in multiple ways. First off, how many levels deep you go will affect how many folders and keywords you can stuff into your URLs. I don't recommend going any deeper than two levels. This will ensure you don't overwhelm your visitors but that you also gain as much as possible in SEO benefits.

Additionally, you will learn how to effectively display and work with the content that you already have. It will create valuable links within your website to other pages in your site.

For example, you'll want to have links across the top of your website that link to the various pages within. Additionally, if you use images for these links, always have text at the bottom of your website that looks like this:

Link | Link | Link | Link

It may be out of the way and no one may ever click on it, but you'll find that the benefit you gain from having keywords with links to specific pages on every page of your website is tremendous.

Keyword Density and Placement

Next up is the density and placement of your keywords throughout the text in your website. Keyword density is more important than ever as Google is getting ever stricter about how much text is too much when you start targeting. Usually a good percentage is between 2 and 4 percent, with

4 being the upper end of what will sound remotely natural in terms of language.

However, in addition to density of your keywords, you also need to consider the placement of the keywords. Keyword placement is important in only a few places, but because certain locations on your website will offer additional prominence for those keywords there are spots where you should always make sure to put them, including:

Headers - The headers of your pages and the titles of the page itself (not the browser window) should always contain keywords.

Subheadings - Secondary headers or even the third or fourth level will still put additional emphasis on your keywords so make sure to put some there as well.

First Paragraph - The earlier keywords appear on your website, the better they will perform, so make sure to get some in the first paragraph or earlier if possible.

Links - As mentioned before, always place keywords within links on your website as they will be more valuable that way.

Make sure to balance the keywords well too - don't stuff all 4% of your keywords in the first 100 words of the text. Always balance them throughout - just make sure to get keywords into those locations if possible.

Inbound Links

Inbound links are the single most important aspect of SEO when you're dealing with Google. They are the basis for the algorithm they use and if you want to rank well for your keywords, you need to get a good number of them pointing to your website.

The first thing to consider is what anchor text is used with those links. Anchor text is the phrase or word that is used to hold the link. For example, a link might look like this: http://www.LINK.com or this: Link

The second one has anchor text of "Link". If that was your keyword, the inbound link here would give you credit for a link coming in for that word. It makes the link more valuable and your site will rank higher for it. There are a few more things to consider as well, including:

The Value of the Link - The link needs to come from a valuable source. That means that getting a link from a page with a Page Rank of 1 or 2 is not going to help you out very much. In fact, this might only hurt your site. Rather, aim for sites with Page Ranks of 3 or higher to link to you.

The Number of Links - The number of links you get for each keyword will greatly benefit you. However, don't misbalance them. While you don't have all that much control over which keywords are used, you should still spend a bit of time trying to get a nice mixture of them for each major keyword on your site.

The more inbound links you get, the better your site will perform. Make sure to build relationships with other site owners, send out lots of viral content and write lots of articles to help build this number up (all things outlined in this book).

Directory Listings

Another way to build up your number of inbound links is to get your site listed in various directories on the Internet. There are two types of directories you can choose from - paid and unpaid.

The paid ones, such as Yahoo! are going to provide higher quality links but are also going to add up very quickly. If you are going to pay for any directory listing, I recommend the Yahoo! directory. If you decide to aim for other paid directories, here is a list of ones that have been effective for many website owners out there:

Business.com - $299 – PR 7 (Page Rank of 7)
Starting Point (www.stpt.com) - $99 - PR 7
Best of the Web (www.botw.org) - $149.95 - PR 7
Ezilon (www.ezilon.com) - $250 - PR 6
WOW Directory (www.wowdirectory.com) - $43 - PR 4
Skaffe (www.skaffe.com) - $29.95 - PR 4
WhatUseek (col.whatuseek.com) - $24.99 - PR 7

But in general, you're going to want to create a long term strategy that uses more free directories than anything else - they are easier to get listed in and they will provide just as many valuable links. The problem only lies in how long it takes to get listed.

Universal Directories - The overarching directories that anyone can be listed in include the likes of DMOZ, the largest directory on the Internet. However, it can take upwards of three to four months to be listed, if not longer when your niche or category is a busy one. Make sure that you submit early here.

Niche Directories - Additionally there are numerous niche directories that can be used as sources of traffic for your website. You will find that these sites will generally be easy to find when you type "Keyword" + "Directory" into the search engine. Whatever your niche is put that in as your directory. You'll be able to get quite a bit of options this way.

I recommend every website to list itself in at least 5-10 directories, whether they are paid or not. There should be plenty of free ones out there to choose from, so always start there if you can.

Indexing and Analytics

Next on the list of valuable SEO tasks to accomplish is indexing and analyzing your content. You want to be sure that you always keep good track of what your website is doing and what you can improve. This is where Google Analytics comes in.

Using Analytics

Google Analytics is a basic, free web service located at http://analytics.google.com. You can login to the service with your Google login and sign up your website for the service fairly easily. Just install the code that they ask for in the bottom of your main page and you'll be able to go in and check in on the content's performance in different time periods.

The most important parts of Analytics though are the reports that tell you how well your website is performing in terms of incoming traffic. Click on "Traffic Sources" and you will see whether you are getting hits from websites, search engines, or direct hits. You will then see how many hits for each source, what keywords were used, how long they stayed on the site, what they clicked on while there and where they went when they were done with your site.

Check to see how your traffic is being generated and then take notes of how you can improve it. If you see that your hits from Google AdWords are staying on the site for an average of 10 minutes, brainstorm how to get those people to convert into sales more often. If you see that you are getting 150 hits a day from a specific keyword, start writing more articles a day for that keyword and blog about it to drum up more traffic.

This information is invaluable in getting the right tweaks put into place to take advantage of your website at the peak of its performance levels.

HTML Structure

The final thing on our top 10 list is the HTML structure of your site. Many people want to go for glitz and glory. I recommend against this as much as possible because in general it will only result in wasted opportunities for your site. You need to be sure that you can effectively fit the keywords into your site as much as possible and that you remove any unneeded clutter from the pages. Here are some tips to keep this from happening:

Less Javascript - Javascript is infamous for cluttering your HTML and watering down your SEO activities. Make sure to put in as little as possible and ensure that you have a good balance of text in there to the code.

No Flash - Don't use Flash if you want to keep text as prominent as possible. Search engines skip over Flash as they have no discernable value for visitors.

Text Instead of Images - Don't use images for text if you can help it. Buttons and banners may look good, but they cut down on how effective you are going to be with the site's SEO campaign.

Clean Text - Keep your text clean and clutter free. This means that you should not use duplicate content from anywhere outside your site, you should not load it down with numbers or unnecessary symbols and you should stick to well written clean content that your visitors can get something out of.

If you use all of these SEO tactics effectively, you're going to find that your website performs better on almost all fronts. The best part is that throughout this book, you'll find dozens of little tricks and tips that are going to add additional value to your website in terms of SEO and beyond. From distributing articles to writing a blog, you'll find that everything you do will ultimately help with SEO if you do it properly and consistently.

Conclusion

The goal of this book has been to show you that there are many more ways to market your business than you have ever been privy to before. From the simplest little strategies like placing ads in search listings to going out of your way to create a series of different articles and blog posts to draw attention and bolster SEO. You're going to get just about everything you could ever hope for out of your business's stint on the Internet if you just use a bit of extra creativity.

Don't ever think that the contents of this book are absolute either. While I'd like to brag that I've covered everything that matters in this day and age (and I'd say I'm pretty close), there are countless other technologies and strategies being developed each day. Just look at a service like Twitter - only a couple of years prior to writing this book, most people had no idea what Twitter was. Today, it is one of the premiere business marketing tools around.

Together with your creativity and drive to succeed, you're going to find that the Internet is a treasure trove of ideas and money making methods. Use them wisely and in conjunction with each other and you will be on the fast track to solid returns in no time flat.

Now that you have been introduced to all these "Insider Strategies" you may be feeling slightly overwhelmed. That's normal. Concentrate on one chapter at a time, one strategy at a time. Soon you will find that you have tackled them all.

Like I said before, these strategies need to be implemented to work. If implemented they <u>will</u> drive traffic. If you can't implement them yourself, pay somebody to do it. Just get it done!

If you need help implementing these strategies in your local small business, that's where I come in. My company, J.P. Marketing, LLC, has a very skilled team that partners with your business to analyze your market, learn your consumers, and take all the necessary steps to optimize your website and insure you are found on the internet.

Call us for a **FREE 24-Point evaluation** ($97 Value) of your website or visit us online and complete the request form. We will review your site, look at potential ways to increase traffic to your site and improve the effectiveness of getting visitors to take action. We will then present our findings plus ask a few more questions about growing your business such as your ability to handle two or three times as much business as you currently experience.

Then if it makes sense, we will create a no obligation proposal identifying ways we can help you achieve your business growth. We like to create win-win situations for our clients and ourselves and for this reason we don't work with every business. We only work with clients we know we can help.

If you'd like to see if your business qualifies for what we have to offer, please request a free evaluation today!

Call us at 800-385-6475

or visit us online at

http://www.SEOAllianceTeam.com